The Horse

The Horse

CANDACE ORD MANROE

MALLARD PRESS

A FRIEDMAN GROUP BOOK

Published by MALLARD PRESS
An Imprint of BDD Promotional Book Company, Inc.
666 Fifth Avenue
New York, NY 10103

Mallard Press and the accompanying duck logo are registered trademarks of BDD Promotional Book Co., Inc. Registered in the U.S. Patent and Trademark Office.

ISBN 0-7924-5755-2

THE HORSE
Legend, Lore, and Everyday Life
was prepared and produced by
Michael Friedman Publishing Group, Inc.
15 West 26th Street
New York, New York 10010

Editor: Dana Rosen
Art Direction: Devorah Levinrad
Designer: Maura Fadden Rosenthal
Photography Editor: Anne K. Price

Typeset by Miller & Debel Typographers, Inc.
Color separations by Scantrans Pte. Ltd.
Printed and bound in Hong Kong by Leefung-Asco Printers Ltd.

To Meagan and Drew and my home state of Texas,
where a love of horses runs deep in the heart.

ACKNOWLEDGMENTS

Elizabeth Niemyer is gratefully acknowledged for allowing us to include works from her exhibition *The Reign of the Horse: The Horse in Print 1500-1715* at the Folger Shakespeare Library in Washington, D.C.

C O N T E N T S

CHAPTER ONE

LORE AND LEGEND
OF THE HORSE

The horse shall be for man a source of happiness and wealth; its back shall be a seat of honor and its belly riches, and every grain of barley given to it shall purchase the indulgence of a sinner to be entered in the register of good works.
Mohammed

Although humans assuredly cast themselves as star in the history they author, a supporting role has long been played by another member of the animal kingdom. Linked to humankind throughout the annals of time is the horse, *Equus caballus* — a half ton of energy, spirit, endurance, and magnificence.

The relationship between humans and horses defies easy categorization, changing radically over time. Primitive humans' attitude toward the primeval horse was anything but sublime. Prehistoric humans hunted the horse, killing colts for food and sparing fillies for future breeding, at which time they would serve as purveyors of milk and, with foals of their own, an even larger food supply. But as humans and horses advanced through evolution, the dynamic

© The Folger Shakespeare Library

changed. By the time of the Greeks, humans weren't regarding the horse as sustenance for the body, but for the soul.

The ancient Greeks must have been astounded when they first glimpsed imported Arabian horses descending from ships and swimming the remaining distance to the Aegean shoreline. What they saw was more than the Arabian's graceful contours and conformation, high tail set and flowing mane, fleet action, and delicate head with dished (concave) profile, tippy ears, and wide-set eyes. The Greeks, who bequeathed what have become the classical aesthetic forms of Western culture, saw in the Arabian a purity of type, an almost Platonic essence of Horse, that their sensibility could not fail to acknowledge.

THIS ENGRAVING FROM JAN SADELER, *PLANETARUM EFFECTUS* (1585), RECOUNTS THE ANCIENT GREEKS' ADMIRATION OF THE HORSE. APOLLO, PROTECTOR OF HERDS AND HERDSMEN, IS SHOWN IN HIS CHARIOT DRAWN BY FOUR LIVELY HORSES.

They promptly added the winged-horse deity, Pegasus (which means "from the water"), to their constellation of supernaturals and set about inscribing his image on every important public edifice, including the most famous building in all of architecture, the Parthenon.

In the millennia before industrialization, entire empires were built on the right proportions of ambition and outstanding steeds—the latter of which were necessary, of course, for charging ambition into battle. Little did the Spanish conquistadors realize the universality of their words when they said, "For, after God, we owed the victory to the horses." Shakespeare, masterful observer of men and manners that he was, knew what he was talking about when he wrote the dialogue for *Richard III:* "A horse! A horse! My kingdom for a horse."

Long the helpmate of common folk, who value their steeds as business partners without whom the job would simply not get done, the horse, defying class bounds, has also been a favorite source of relaxation, rejuvenation, and pure pleasure for aristocracy, royalty, and rulers.

Napoleon, perhaps in an attempt to disprove the limitations of his stature, rode into battle only on an ill-tempered stallion of a height more appropriate as mount for a much taller individual. Benjamin Disraeli, prime minister of Britain in the last half of the nineteenth century, was unabashedly optimistic about the horse as an elixir for any problem: "A canter," he said, "is the cure for every evil." In modern times, it's hard to think of Charles, Prince of Wales, merely as heir to the British throne: the prince's affection for his polo ponies cuts too intriguing and humanizing an image to ignore.

As humankind's constant counterpart throughout history, the horse may be regarded as an equalizer. Just as the horse was and is owned and appreciated by all echelons of society from plebian to privileged, so has it bridged the gap between genders. While brandishing warriors into battle, this same animal was being ridden or driven by the women left behind.

And the women weren't always left behind. Queen Isabella of Spain, descendant of Alfred the Great and John of Gaunt, and whose daughter married Henry VIII, was one of the world's greatest equestriennes. A rider from age three, she shunned the mules that society expected her to ride and went galloping, instead, on a horse. Isabella attended her coronation wearing white brocade and riding (what else?) a white horse. Traveling on horseback for hundreds of miles through all kinds of menacing weather conditions, she helped her husband in his military campaigns, clothed in armor over a lightweight dress.

Isabella's influence on the equestrian world is incalculable. She refined the important stud farms of Andalusia, encouraging development of the Arabian bloodline. As the patroness of Columbus, who reintroduced horses to the New World after millions of years of absence, Isabella must be given due credit for the spread of the horse into those new quarters. She fiercely supported the expedition, volunteering to sell all her jewels and her crown itself to finance the voyage. (It must be assumed that this offer to divest herself of her jeweled possessions even included a willingness to part with her favorite pearl-embroidered riding shirt, as well as the bridle and saddle of gold, which Isabella enlisted for the ride to mass each week.)

© Saskia Ltd.

Top left: The horse figures in mythology and popular folklore not only in regard to its relation with men. Some of the most legendary equine tales of all time include women, as attested by Lady Godiva. Top Right: Revered by the British, the Andalusian is believed to have been Shakespeare's model for Adonis' mount in *Venus and Adonis*, a narrative poem rich in horse allusion. Shown here is a print from *Equini Generis, Animalis inter Quadrapedes Nobilissimi* by Jan van der Straet (c. 1580).

Women weren't accorded the same set of rules for riding as men, but ride they did. Impoverished women rode sidesaddle, if lucky enough to have access to a horse at all. Even today, in some poorer parts of the Mediterranean region and Ireland, peasant women can be seen riding sideways on the rump of a pony. Women of privilege and pedigree rode atop a whirlicote, which protected their clothing, while their feet rested on a board.

Erstwhile Greek maidens were said to ride naked to facilitate ease with childbirth. Their legendary ancestors, the Amazons (which means "without breasts"), were great horsewomen who also killed their sons at birth.

And in contemporary times, anyone who has spent any time at all at a riding stable can attest that, if a boy and his dog make a poignant pair, then a girl and her horse are at least as dynamic a duo.

The role of the horse is often mythological, sometimes scandalous. Catherine the Great, who ruled Russia in the late eighteenth century, is reported to have had an unnatural affection for the stallions in her stable. Lady Godiva's fame in our folklore would have been far less prominent had her nudity not been exhibited from the back of a horse. One need look no further than literature and film to discover our mythical association of the horse: the Black Stallion, Black Beauty, National Velvet, Silver, and Flicka all have a larger-than-life dimension—indeed, a larger-than-life-in-cinema dimension—that attests to our seemingly insatiable desire to romance the equine realm. Grammy-winning songwriter/musician Lyle Lovett summed it up best in these lyrics: "And if I was Roy Rogers, I'd sure enough be single. I couldn't bring myself to marrying old Dale. It'd just be me and Trigger. We'd go riding through them movies...."

What is it about the horse, then, that appeals to individuals as different as the Marlboro man and manicured royalty? What is it that allures old and young, male and female, backwoods down-homer and urban sophisticate alike? What is it about this mammal that makes a female rancher in Texas swear she would lose her mind with the day-in, day-out tedium of ranch operations were it not for her daily morning ride? (Ostensibly, that sunrise ride is to check fence lines, but she confides, "Really, it's therapy.")

What is it, finally, that convinces an editor like myself to shed corporate uniform for jeans and boots, in order to spend an extended weekday lunch hour picking mud and manure from a horse's hooves under the hot sun in air fresh with flies and caliche dust?

When early humans first encountered the horse as something more than a potential food source, the fundamental appeal was still likely to have been related to function: here was a four-legged beast, not completely docile but certainly not vicious, large enough and amply powerful to serve as a conveyor for humans themselves, as well as their burdens—even into battle.

But perhaps prehistoric humans shouldn't be short-sold. However primitive and pragmatic their instincts, is it not possible that they shared some semblance of the sensibilities that characterize today's horse lover? How could it be otherwise, as their mounts eventually accepted them on their backs, moved forward at their prompting, and carried them with an energy and pent-up power that manifested as rippling muscles and a hardy lather along the neck and shoulders? With the wind whipping by, trees and enemies left in a trail of dusty tracks, early humans propelled by horse must have experienced something close to joy.

ABOVE: IN PONDERING HUMANKIND'S ADMIRATION OF THE HORSE, ONE NEED LOOK NO FARTHER THAN THE ANIMAL ITSELF. PHYSICALLY, THE HORSE IS AMONG THE MOST AESTHETICALLY PLEASING OF ALL CREATURES IN THE ANIMAL KINGDOM. BELOW: MANY AN EQUESTRIAN TAKES CONSOLATION IN THE PRESENCE OF A HORSE, WHETHER IN THE SADDLE OR OFF, MERELY REVELING IN THE ANIMAL'S MAJESTIC BEAUTY.

DEFINING THE PREHISTORIC HORSE

To understand how the horse was tamed by humans, it is imperative to first know something about the prehistoric horse as a discrete consideration unto itself.

The Dawn Horse

The earliest ancestor of the horse was a tiny creature that inhabited the earth sixty million years ago. This animal was known as eohippus, which means the "dawn horse," taken from the two Greek words, *eos* (dawn) and *hippus* (horse). Interestingly, the creature's original habitat was North America, from which it later disappeared and reappeared only with the arrival of the Spanish conquistadors. At the time of its evolution, the dawn horse was able to travel freely across land bridges connecting North America to Asia, as well as to Africa and Europe. After the Ice Age, when sea levels rose, this free range was cut off.

Until a little more than one hundred years ago, nothing was known about this ancestor of the modern horse. But in 1869, when the Union Pacific Railroad

was laying tracks across Wyoming, crews unearthed strange bones, which they gave to the Smithsonian Institution. Subsequent scientific studies revealed these casually found bones to be the ancestor of the horse—eohippus.

Eohippus stood no more than about a foot (30 cm) high and struck a closer resemblance to today's small dog than to the modern horse. The earliest fossils of eohippus show it as having four legs and feet, with each front foot having four toes, and each hind foot having three toes. Each toe, peculiarly, ended in a tiny hoof of its own. It is believed that an even earlier version of eohippus existed, though no fossils have been exhumed as documentation. This earlier version on the evolutionary chart is believed to have had, like man, five toes on each foot. Further, it is thought to have had teeth like a monkey, for browsing (eating from trees), rather than grazing (eating grass from the ground, as does today's *Equus caballus*).

In the 1920s, an archaeological dig by students from Iowa State University came across an important find: the first complete skeleton of eohippus. Before that, only miscellaneous bones and body parts had been located. Study of this intact dawn horse, found in Bighorn County, Wyoming, enabled scientists to shed incredible light on our understanding of the development of the horse.

The dawn horse's toes, being so clearly foreign to our modern understanding of the horse, were a subject of intense interest. Scientists surmised that as tiny eohippus locomoted about, it relied more on the middle toes of all its feet than on any of the other toes. As a result of this heavy use, the middle toe grew larger over time; the other toes, so little used, atrophied and grew smaller, eventually just hanging uselessly beside the strong middle toe.

Over millions of years, the dawn horse slowly grew in size, eventually approaching the height of a zebra. Excavations in Idaho along the Snake River in the 1930s revealed bones of this zebra-sized dawn horse, along with fossils of water-loving creatures such as beavers, frogs, and fish. What is now an arid, rocky, forbidding terrain, then, must have once been hospitably blessed with water—a necessary condition, it can be concluded, for the existence of the dawn horse.

EOHIPPUS, MEANING THE ''DAWN HORSE,'' IS THE EARLIEST KNOWN ANCESTOR OF THE MODERN HORSE. IT STOOD ABOUT ONE FOOT (30 CM) TALL AND INHABITED NORTH AMERICA ABOUT SIXTY MILLION YEARS AGO.

As mentioned, the dawn horse had an incredible range over several present-day continents, thanks to land bridges linking these now-separated landmasses. This proved to be a good thing. Inexplicably, some 11,000 to 8,000 years ago, all of the horses in the Western world vanished, due to plague, disease, or death at the hands of primitive humans. Whatever the reason, the result was that *Equus caballus* evolved from the dawn horse in Europe, Asia, and Africa, and not North America.

FROM DAWN TO DOMESTIC: ANCIENT PROTOTYPES OF THE MODERN HORSE

It is a long way from the dawn horse to today's domestic horse, with much equine evolutionary change and innumerable interpretations by humans in the interim.

For most of recorded history, it was believed that the domestic horse derived from a single source (a monophyletic theory). Even Darwin, espousing his ideas of evolution and natural selection regarding the horse, believed that it descended from one origin only. Until the turn of the twentieth century, in fact, only one theory of multiple sources (polyphyletic) had been advanced.

That polyphyletic theory was conceptualized by Hamilton Smith, who said that the domestic horse actually had several ancestors in the wild, as evidenced by the variety of colors of the domestic horse's coat. Since articulating his theory, Smith has been proven wrong on its specifics—contemporary color of coat has nothing to do with the original ancestry of the domestic horse. But in the general vein, Smith was on target: the idea of more than one type of ancestor in the wild is the theory, reformulated and made increasingly sophisticated, that is most widely held today.

In an article published in 1904 in *Nature*, Edinburgh's J. Cossar Ewart presented the results of his hybridization experiments with Equidae and his studies of the early horse. Here, he articulated the idea of the domestic horse having several progenitors.

These earliest ancestors included what Ewart called the Celtic pony, the heavier Norse horse of the North, the wild Mongolian horse (known as the Przewalski—an early type discovered in 1881 and, at that time, held to be the sole source of all domestic horses), two other unnamed horse-sized ancestors (one with a straight head, the other with a ram's head), and the small or pony-sized cline (a later term used to describe this ancestor that Ewart identified as begetting the Arabian, as well as the Welsh and Exmoor ponies).

According to Ewart, these major types weren't confined to any narrow region but were widely distributed. In addition, he postulated that several of the prototypes possibly coexisted within a single geographical district.

Today, although there are still some who support a single-ancestor theory, the greatest consensus favors a plurality of parentage. With the benefit of more sophisticated archaeological tools such as carbon-14 dating, however, today's

© Sally Klein

THE REGAL LIPIZZANER, ALONG WITH ALL OTHER BREEDS OF MODERN HORSES, WAS FOR YEARS BELIEVED TO HAVE EVOLVED FROM A SINGLE SOURCE. CURRENT THEORY, HOWEVER, TRACES HORSE ANCESTRY TO SEVERAL DIFFERENT HORSE TYPES, WHICH WERE FOUND IN DIFFERENT REGIONS OF THE WORLD.

proponents of a multi-ancestral theory have revised Ewart's original concept somewhat, coming up with four basic types of horses and a somewhat later fifth type, which is a cross between two of the originals.

This newest polyphyletic scheme, using Ewart's theory as a launching point, is a distillation of the works of Speed, Skorkowski, Ebhardt, and d'Andrade from, respectively, Scotland, Poland, Germany, and Portugal. Ewart's Celtic pony from northwest Europe remains on the latest list of lineage, as does his heavier Norse horse from northern Eurasia.

A third type of ancient predecessor of the domestic horse is believed to be from Central Asia, extending westward north of the Alps as far as Spain. This type is thought to have contributed to the Nisaean and Bactrian breeds and, in part, to the Thoroughbred. A fourth type included in the modern view is a western Asian pony, fine-boned with a straight or concave head and only about twelve hands tall—similar to the recently identified Caspian and believed by some schools to be ancestor to the Arabian (possibly even via a cross with a zebra).

THE FIRST HORSES WERE TOO SMALL TO ACCOMMODATE RIDERS UPON THEIR BACKS AND THEREFORE WERE DOMESTICATED FOR PULLING CONVEYANCES INSTEAD. AS THE ANIMAL EVOLVED TO A LARGER SIZE, HOWEVER, HUMANS TOOK ADVANTAGE OF THE OPPORTUNITY FOR MORE DIRECT CONTACT, AS CERTAIN PETROGLYPHS ATTEST.

© Spencer Swanger/Tom Stack and Associates

A final type, Tarpans, represented a cross between types one and four. Ewart's Przewalski is not on the list; later evidence rules it out based on a chromosome count that differs from all other domestic horses.

But really, the multi-origin theory requires virtually no leap of faith. Prehistoric cave drawings point to a number of quite different varieties of ancient horses. On the roof of the cave of Rouffignac in the Dordogne, paintings show horses that greatly resemble today's Exmoor pony. A drawing that embellishes a cave at Niaux in the Pyrenees, on the other hand, shows a large, looming horse that resembles a Clydesdale more than anything. Other examples of cave art depicting discrepancies in the appearance of horses point to the presence of more than one horse type in early times.

So, with the working assumption that early man domesticated not just one type of horse but several different types or species, how did the process look? How did it get started and why? Was the process the same for all horses domesticated? How much time was involved—could it have been an amount comparable to that required to break a horse to saddle today, with our current knowledge and training?

THE SUPPLE ATHLETICISM, AESTHETIC CONFORMATION, AND FINE SPIRIT EXHIBITED BY ANY NUMBER OF BREEDS OF HORSES IN TODAY'S SHOW RING ARE THE RESULTS OF YEARS OF CONSCIENTIOUS, SCIENTIFIC BREEDING.

© Sally Klein

ABOVE: THIS SCENE FROM ADRIAAN HOFFER'S
NEDERDUYTSCHE POËMATA (1635) SHOWS HOW
BEFORE THE INVENTION OF THE TRACTOR, THE
HORSE WAS AN IMPORTANT LABOR SOURCE IN
AGRICULTURE. OPPOSITE PAGE: A HISTORY OF
CAVALRY TACTICS IS SHOWN IN HERMAN HUGO'S
DE MILITIA EQUESTRI ANTIQUA ET NOVA (1630).

DOMESTICATION: FROM REINDEER TO REINING HORSES

It is known that the horse was being domesticated by humans as early as 3000 B.C., though it's not currently possible to get any more precise than that. As our archaeological data accumulates and our dating techniques grow more sophisticated, however, it seems likely that we may find tangible evidence pointing to encounters between humans and beast in the early part of that millenium.

The question of where domestication began must be addressed with as much latitude and flexibility as the task of fixing a date. Did domestication begin with one people, in one region of the planet, and then spread to other cultures? Or did horsemen spontaneously emerge across the globe, each culture befriending the animal on its own, with no awareness of other efforts? Theories exist to support both ideas, but the most plausible explanation would seem to be a combination of the two, with both cultural exchange and isolated spontaneity responsible for the spread of domestication.

What is known with some measure of certainty is that the event occurred northeast of the Mediterranean (though some sources hold Egypt as the cradle of domestication), possibly as far away as the hinterlands of outermost Siberia, near the shoreline of the Bering Strait, and at least as distant as the Oxus (Amu Darya) basin. The geographic location can't be narrowed beyond that.

Although it's impossible to say for sure, the first horse to be tamed and put into humans' service was probably the type-two, or Norse, horse. This animal's habitat included northeast Asia—an area that also happened to be home to reindeer. Ancient people of that region are known to have domesticated reindeer, which they mounted and rode and also used to drive sleighlike contraptions. One tribe, the Yakuts, even continue to employ reindeer in this fashion today.

Logic says that it would have been a short step for these aboriginal people to move from being domesticators of reindeer to domesticators of horses—at least, it would be easier than attempting to tame horses with no expertise whatsoever. However difficult the task, the aboriginal tribes tamed the horse to work under saddle or in front of a sleigh, not to drive conveyances with wheels—for wheels did not come to northeast Asia until much later.

The type-two horse wasn't merely an aid in peaceful labor, however. It was soon prized as a human's partner in war. Archers living in eastern Siberia, Mongolia, and Manchuria enlisted the animal to carry them, charging with double-curved bows into battle, as they invaded to the west. And as the archers pressed onward into new regions, suffering loss in battle, they needed to replenish their stock. This resulted in other species of horses being added to the herd of the type-two. The battles in which these horses participated became particularly intense under the Turks, who used horses to drive chariots, the Scythians, with their famous composite bow, and, at the time of Christ, the Parthians. Horseback warring in Europe—which most likely got its start with the domestication of the type-two horse—continued almost until the beginning of the eighteenth century.

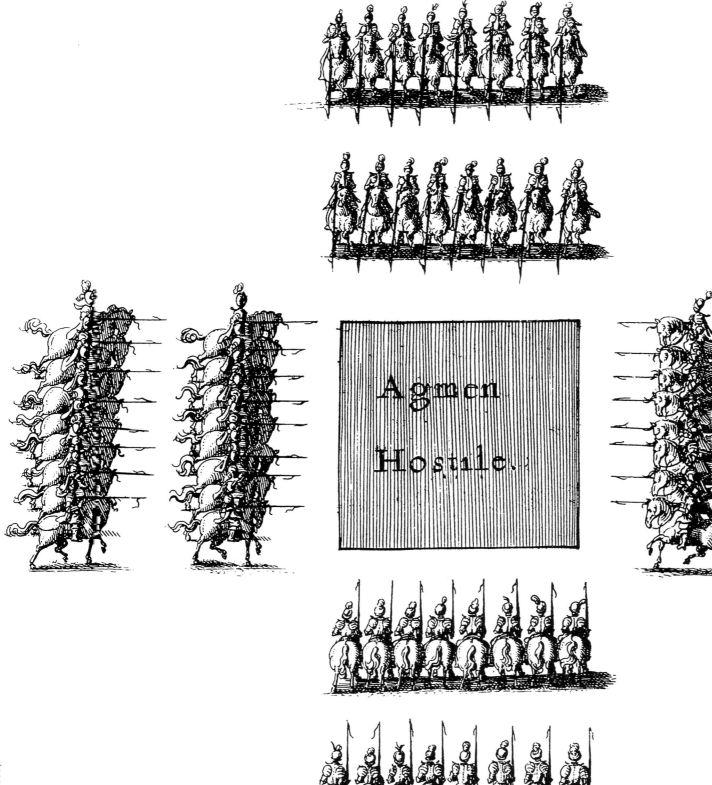

THE MUSCULAR POWER OF THE HORSE HAS
CAPTURED ARTISTS' EYES THROUGH THE AGES.
THIS ILLUSTRATION IS FROM THE FIRST BOOK ON
THE ANATOMY OF THE HORSE, CARLO RUINI'S
ANATOMIA DEL CAVALLO (1618).

Chariots of Fire

The type-one, or Celtic pony, as Ewart had called it, was actually domesticated by the Celts' predecessors in northwest Europe—people such as Scotland's Picts and Scandinavia's Norse ancestors, for instance. Cave art from the Bronze Age found in Scandinavia reveals the type-one pony poised in pairs before a chariot. Its physique made it capable of having a swift trot, as well as an energetic and spirited action, both of which lent themselves well to chariot driving.

The Celts, for whom the type-one pony is named, first domesticated an altogether different horse, the Tarpan, which was a cross between type-one and type-four horses. The Tarpan was the dominant primeval breed in the lower Danube valley, where the Celts lived, and the Celtic chariots, therefore, were first drawn by this breed, and not by the type-one Celtic pony. That came later.

Around 500 B.C. the Celts began their exodus from the Danube, doing battle along the way and acquiring considerable quantities of horses in the process. By the time they were ready to invade Britain, then, the Celts not only had the Tarpan, a mix of two horse types, but also several others as well. These horses that the Celts brought with them were then bred with the aboriginal animals, making the ancient animal we think of now as the Celtic pony. The early Celtic pony is well represented by the modern-day Exmoor, as proven by the Exmoor's successful driving of an ancient British chariot unearthed in Wales.

Thinking Tall

The type-three horse, including the extremely tall, famous Nisaean breed, began appearing in Europe with the Persian invasions of Macedonia. Under Alexander the Great, the horses were claimed for Macedonia during its conquest of the Persian empire. Helping with the conquest were Bactrian horsemen, who had been conquered earlier by Alexander. Both the Bactrian and Nisaean animals, then, comprised type-three, the ancestor of the Thoroughbred.

Proto-Arabian

This small type-four horse, though capable of aiding humans as transportation and load bearer, was probably not put through the same rigors of battle that its prehistoric kin were required to face. The animal was simply too small to be an effectively fast and pernicious charger.

It can't be determined exactly when humans first tamed the type-four—the prototype of the breed to be called, many centuries later, the Arabian. It was after Alexander the Great's empire was crumbling that the type-four horse started to become plentiful in Mediterranean Europe.

The earlier-mentioned possibility that a zebra and a horse crossed to produce this fourth horse type is not as unreasonable as it might sound, when it is realized that zebras themselves, despite their lack of withers, have been domesticated. What is more amazing is the thought that this possible parentage produced, eventually, the Arabian—the single most influential and pure breed today, whose genes of strength, beauty, and grace have left a notable impact on the bloodlines of many other derivative breeds.

A Riding Relationship

When humans first got around to domesticating the horse, it wasn't the directly tactile, skin-to-skin experience it might have been. In most instances, the early horse was too small to be mounted; instead, it was tamed to pull a wheeled device or a sleigh. Humans had yet to experience the singular feeling of direct contact with an animal of considerable power and a mind of its own.

The earliest record we have of a human actually riding a horse is an engraving on a bone from Susa in the third millennium B.C. An Egyptian figurine from 1580 B.C. on the tomb of Horenhab shows a horse ridden by a groom, proving that horseback riding had reached Egypt or developed there by that date. Likewise, a Mycenaean clay figurine dating some 250 years later shows that, by this time, horseback riding had reached Greece.

For a long time, no texts recorded any information on riding. Certainly the Old Testament offered little insight to the horse's domestication—for the Israelites held a taboo against the steed, associating it with Egyptians and Assyrians until the time of Solomon. The great patriarchs rode camels or donkeys, not horses, and the Bible has little information to offer on equine matters until around 900 B.C. Other sources document the existence of domestic horses by that time, anyway, diluting the importance of the biblical data. Similarly, Greek and Latin classics from 800 B.C. are too late, in terms of when domestication of the horse occurred, to shed much light on the topic.

Artifacts—prehistoric bas-relief carvings, pottery, sculpture, and cave drawings—are all that's available to fill in the gaps left by a paucity of books. Some of this evidence of humans riding horses is detailed enough to identify breed. Such is the case with a statue in a British museum of a Libyan woman riding what easily can be identified today as an Arabian horse, with its characteristic high tail set and dished face. An oral tradition rife with legend and myth involving the horse substantiates the ancient artifacts as further proof of humans' riding relationship with the horse.

The earliest serious text on the subject did not appear until 1360 B.C. This document, *The Chariot Training Manual* of Kikkulis the Mittanite, was not about riding a horse, however, as much as it was about training the animal for chariot driving.

Until the time of Xenophon the Greek, then, no specific textual information was recorded that is extant today on how to go about riding from the back of a horse.

THE HORSE DIDN'T SIMPLY APPEAR TO HUMANS ONE DAY WITH A HALTER AND LEAD ROPE AROUND ITS HEAD AND NECK, WAITING TO BE TIED TO A HITCHING POST. EQUINE DOMESTICATION WAS A PROCESS, ONE THAT THE EARLIEST DOMESTICATORS PROBABLY WERE SOMEWHAT PREPARED FOR AS A RESULT OF THEIR DOMESTICATION OF THE REINDEER.

Xenophon, born in Athens in 430 B.C., served in the Greek army under Cyrus and was elected to lead ten thousand soldiers in a two-year getaway. As an equestrian, he learned from the richer horsemanship traditions of the Persians and Armenians, who were great hunters of the 800s B.C. These observations and gems of wisdom were shared by Xenophon in two books, *Hippike* and *Hipparchikos*, written after his retirement for his two sons, who also were in the cavalry.

In the books, Xenophon describes mounting Persian-style with a leg up—what has long since been accepted as the standard mounting technique in English equitation. He also suggests working horses downhill as the Persians did—another training exercise commonly used today—and he described the first "horseshoe": a strip of cloth covering the hoof and tied above the fetlock for protection from abrasive rocks and dangerous ice.

Xenophon is considered the founder of classical equitation—of modern horsemanship—and most of his directives are still respected and followed by riders today. Xenophon sagely warned, for example, to instruct a horse with reward, associating good behavior with something the horse likes, be it food or rest; inappropriate behavior from the animal, he advised, best be promptly countered with a reprimand. Xenophon covered all topics of horsemanship, including buying, breaking, and schooling horses. He taught balancing and suppling exercises that demanded changes in direction and pace and involved circles and turns.

One major difference between Xenophon's prowess with equines and present-day horsemanship, however, does exist: that difference emanates from Xenophon's lack of a saddle. He rode bareback, with long, extended legs and turned-down toes, on the premise that a human's naked legs provided the most adhesion to the horse's sweating coat.

This adhesion wasn't sufficient for battle, however. And it was not until the fourth century A.D. that the situation changed. At that time, the Huns of Mongolia invented the stirrup, a turning point after which the development of horsemanship advanced with amazing swiftness.

The Middle Ages brought a high degree of schooling for the horse with jousts and tournaments by mounted knights. But it wasn't until the Renaissance period of 1500 to 1600 that riding was recognized as an art form in its own right, of a caliber with music, literature, and the other fine arts. At this period, it became imperative for nobility to ride and ride well.

Frenchman François Robichon de la Gueriniere (1688–1751), who came to be known as the father of classical equitation, had enormous influence. It was mainly due to his teachings that two monumental schools of classical equitation were formed in Europe: the French schools of Versailles and Saumur, and the Spanish Riding School of Vienna, famous even today for its flying Lipizzaners. Basic to de la Gueriniere's technique was a system of suppling and gymnastic exercises, including his invention of the shoulder-in, that were designed to develop and accentuate the horse's natural movements and gaits. In addition, he stressed minimal use of artificial aids to get the horse to perform. Instead of inflicting pain on the animal, he urged the rider to learn to use his or her own body in subtle, refined movements to discreetly cue the horse a command.

A STUDY FOR THE SFORZA MONUMENT BY LEONARDO DA VINCI (C. 1490).

THE HORSE

Little documentation can be found regarding the Spanish Riding School's early years, but it is known that the school officially opened in 1735 at the bequest of Emperor Charles VI. A brochure from 1833 stated that "The Imperial Royal Court Riding School accepts trainees only by special permission of the Office of the Chief Master of the Horses, and every day you can ride your own horse there between the hours of twelve and three in the afternoon." But after 1894, the school was extremely exclusive, open only to officers and aristocracy committed to Haute Ecole and willing to pay exorbitant fees in its pursuit.

After 1918, when the Austro-Hungarian monarchy collapsed, the future of the school became uncertain. It was taken into state control, and thanks to the publicity efforts of its chief rider, Moritz Herold, began its first public performances in July 1920. The tradition has continued even into the present, with the highly schooled Lipizzaners performing the classical art of equitation in the school's original facility—the only such facility remaining dedicated to the art.

THUNDERING ACROSS A NEW WORLD

FROM THE TIME OF EOHIPPUS' DISAPPEARANCE DURING THE ICE AGE UNTIL COLUMBUS' REINTRODUCTION OF HORSES, THE NEW WORLD WAS ENTIRELY VOID OF THE ANIMAL.

The thunder of horse hooves pummeling prairie grass or forest glade was a sound unknown to the New World for eons, until Columbus' second voyage to America. For his first trip in 1492, he had brought along no mounts. But before venturing back a second time, he had the foresight to request Queen Isabella of Spain to purvey him with horses.

His wish was granted in grand style. Queen Isabella gave Columbus twenty-five of the finest Arabians to be found in her royal stables. But legend has it that the soldiers traded their fine Arabians for drink and food, before ever taking to the sea. By the time they departed on their voyage, the horses they had to bring along were nags of no special importance whatsoever. And it was these, it is believed, that were the first horses to inhabit America since the Ice Age.

In 1518, Hernando Cortéz and his eighteen-man cavalry brought horses with them from Spain for the purpose of laying siege to Mexico. Twenty-one years later, Hernando de Soto arrived in North America, docking in what is now Florida, with a sizable herd of some 300 horses. The following year, in 1540, Francisco Vásquez de Coronado brought 250 horses along on his expedition to the Rio Grande country of North America, where the horses ranged over Mexico, Texas, and Arizona, and as far northeast as Kansas.

Some of these large herds no doubt ran their own course, living and breeding in the wild. Certainly by the time the Spanish colonists began arriving in number, horses were plentiful in North America. By 1570, huge herds roamed all over the prairie lands of the Southwest and Mexico, even up to the Canadian border.

The breed of horse imported most often by the Spanish to America was probably Arabian. The Spanish shipped these horses to Cuba, Santo Domingo, the Antilles, and Jamaica, expressly for the purpose of supplying them to the conquistadors, who soon no longer needed to transport them from Spain.

CHAPTER TWO

OWNERSHIP:
ROMANCE AND REALITY

© Bob Winsett/Tom Stack & Associates

Far back, far back in our dark soul the horse prances....The horse, the horse! The symbol of surging potency and power of movement, of action, in man.

D.H. Lawrence, Apocalypse

Dan Dry/Visions

ABOVE: HORSE OWNERS SHOULD NOT HAVE
FOOLISH EXPECTATIONS THAT AFFECTION IN-
EVITABLY WILL BE FORTHCOMING FROM A HORSE.
A WISER EXPECTATION WOULD BE PERFORMANCE
AND TRUST. OPPOSITE PAGE, TOP: HORSE FEVER
TYPICALLY STRIKES THE VERY YOUNG, AS EVI-
DENCED BY THIS CHILD RIDING THE BARRELS IN A
CHILDREN'S RODEO EVENT. OPPOSITE PAGE,
BOTTOM: MINIATURE HORSES ARE UNDERGOING
A BURGEONING POPULARITY, BUT ONLY AS ODDI-
TIES FOR SHOW OR AS PETS, BECAUSE THEY
CANNOT BE USED FOR ACTIVITIES THAT DEMAND
RIDING.

Equine lore is steeped in romance—a fact that, coupled with the intrinsic magne-
tism of the animal itself, makes it easy for otherwise sane beings to become driven
by an obsessive impulse to buy a horse of their own. And should horse fever strike
the young, it's especially potent, the only sure antidote being implacable parents.

For as long as I can remember, the iconography of my heart has been shaped
like a horse.

As a child, I looked forward to those times once or twice a year when we
would drive from our home in the city to my uncle's horse farm for family retreats.
The air was fresher, the grass greener, and thanks to the horses, life inifinitely

more interesting, charged with power and possibility. Of course the drive back to the city was miserable for my parents. The childish chant of the earlier trip changed from, "Are we there yet?" to, "May I get a horse?" on the return. This was a refrain to be repeated — and resolutely denied — many times during subsequent years of pestering and protestation.

For the child hopelessly in love with horses, it's impossible to entertain the thought that there might be good reason *not* to own a horse. Desire dismisses reason, leaves logic at a fast trot. What I couldn't see as a young girl blinded by love was that my parents were absolutely right: the horse is no ordinary pet. At that time in my life, I had no business owning one.

Before making the major decision to buy a horse, it's important to strip away the romanticism and take a hard look at what's really involved. Owning a horse is not the same as owning a house pet.

© Richard Day

The initial investment—the cash on the table—is high, and that's only the beginning. Whereas all pets require ongoing attention and entail a certain amount of expense, the horse surpasses most other domestic creatures on both counts. Stable, veterinarian, farrier, tack, training, grooming aids, and feed bills make the horse a reality of a much different magnitude. Like a highly refined European sports car, the horse costs more up front, but it's the hidden price tag of maintenance that drives it into a rarefied realm, beyond reason for some.

Unless your budget can accommodate not only the up-front purchase price but the ongoing care, it's best to leave horse ownership in the hands of those with more disposable income. Cheating the horse out of care it needs—hooves trimmed by the farrier or teeth floated by the vet—is unconscionable, no matter how great the desire for a horse of your own.

ABOVE: EXERCISE IS IMPORTANT TO A HORSE'S HEALTH AND FITNESS. IF RIDING ON A REGULAR BASIS IS NOT POSSIBLE, ANOTHER FORM OF EXERCISE SHOULD BE PROVIDED FOR THE HORSE CONFINED TO A STALL. THIS THOROUGHBRED IS BEING EXERCISED ON AN AUTOMATIC HOT WALKER. RIGHT: UNLIKE A HOUSEHOLD PET, A HORSE IS A HIGH-MAINTENANCE ANIMAL. A VISIT FROM THE FARRIER TO APPLY NEW SHOES OR TRIM THE HOOVES IS ONLY ONE OF THE SERVICES THAT MUST BE PROVIDED TO KEEP THE HORSE SOUND. FARRIERS, LIKE VETS, CHARGE FOR STABLE CALLS, WHICH MAY BE A FACTOR IN DECIDING WHETHER TO BOARD A HORSE BY ITSELF OR AT A FACILITY WITH OTHER HORSES. AT A STABLE, THE "HOUSE CALL" CAN BE SHARED BY OTHER HORSE OWNERS.

© Richard Day

TIME

UNLESS ICE MAKES FOOTING DANGEROUS, HORSES CAN BE RIDDEN ANY TIME OF YEAR. THE ONLY DETERRENT IS THE RIDER, WHO MAY BE LESS WILLING TO BRAVE A SNOWY WINTER THAN IS THE HORSE. FOR THIS RIDER IN RIVERTON, WYOMING, SNOW IS NO OBSTACLE.

Expense is the only the first difference distinguishing the horse from house pets. A related requirement is time: to have a relationship with a horse, you must invest of yourself—of your time—on a regular basis.

A trip once every other week to the stable for a quick ride at your convenience does not produce a horse highly attuned and sensitized to your cues as rider. And it's not just the horse that suffers. You won't reap the rewards of a ride made in heaven—for what the horse lacks from the infrequency of your visits you assuredly will feel in its ride.

Frequent short visits, even if they entail only twenty minutes of schooling your horse in an arena, are better than infrequent long sessions. Contact and reinforcement are what matter most, although your horse will learn better and be happier if you can combine frequent schooling with pure pleasure rides on the trail.

If your schedule is already demanding and there doesn't appear to be much free time for horsemanship, it would be wise to postpone purchasing a horse until circumstances have altered. Not only is an absentee owner unfair to the horse, it's unfair to the owner as well, who is sure to accrue at least some degree of guilt for the untended animal.

© Mark E. Gibson

While addressing the issues of money and time, one equally critical question must be answered: where will you put the horse? In most instances, this doesn't pose too great a problem. Even in the city, stables are available, though finding a good one that's convenient and affordable and that still has an open stall for your horse may be more difficult than you imagined.

Not unlike a child-care facility, a stable requires the same kind of inspection by the prospective client. A poorly managed stable with ill-fed and ill-watered horses and filthy stalls is a horse owner's nightmare. Finding a good one at the outset is by far the most attractive option.

Clean, dry bedding is a must, as is adequate drainage, especially if the stalls open onto outdoor runs. This requirement is not just for the horse's comfort but for its health, in order to prevent the hoof disease, called thrush, which is caused by continual dampness. Good fencing and stall-building materials are important if injury to the animal is to be avoided. Other features, such as automatic watering mechanisms for each stall, and horse shower stalls for the barn, are selling points but not necessities for a good stable.

The more selective you are, the more difficulty you may have finding an acceptable facility. Ideally, good-sized box stalls opening onto runs provide the animal with natural light, fresh air, and an opportunity for mobility and moderate exercise. A stall plus regular or even daily turnout into pasture works well for owners who aren't obsessive about keeping their horses free from nicks for the show ring, but this best-of-both-worlds compromise is contingent upon geography: some urban stables simply don't have access to pastureland. Many stables offer daily exercise among their amenities, thus negating the necessity for pasture turnout—but this service is not inexpensive.

Pasturing a horse all of the time, with no stall, is another option. One attractive benefit is that this arrangement costs about half as much as boarding in a barn. But you must be sure that the pasture isn't overcrowded (a rule of thumb allots one horse per acre [.4 ha]), that the grasses are lush and not toxic, and that the land is decently maintained, free from loose barbed wire and unfilled ruts that could cause injury to the animal.

One of the most traumatic experiences I have had as a horse owner resulted from a poorly maintained pasture. A jagged tree stump perforated my horse's pastern as he raced along the fence line, spilling his synovial fluid, producing a temporary lameness, risking long-term arthritic problems, and causing permanent cosmetic damage that, should I ever decide to sell, would lower the animal's market value. All that—in addition to the initial sleepless night at the stable, waiting to see if the antibiotics would kick in and kill early infection.

Another caution regarding year-round pasturing is climate: severe winters take their toll on pastured horses, in appearance if not in health. If you plan to show during the winter, a stall is probably your best bet. Shaggy winter coats seldom seduce judges in the show ring.

THE HORSE

One more point to take into account before choosing to pasture is winter feeding. When the grass is gone, hay and grain feedings aren't merely ancillary, but imperative. If your pasture care does not include auxiliary feedings, be sure you can do the feeding yourself before committing your horse to pasture.

EMOTIONAL PAYOFF

It should be clear by now that the horse requires a great deal more money, time, and care than do most animals typically thought of as pets. With all that effort, it would seem that an emotional payoff should be in order. The truth is, your horse cannot be relied upon to bond with you in the sycophantic fashion of a dog. Horses typically do not grieve for their owners, nor do they travel long distances in search of them, tracking their scent.

One of the greatest disappointments I've witnessed among riders occurred when a woman in her early forties paid a healthy sum for a young Arabian filly she wanted as her special friend. Every morning and every evening without fail, the woman would come to the stable to groom the horse, daub fly repellent around its eyes and ears, and coo and kiss its neck and muzzle. Clearly this cloying behavior agitated the filly, which would toss its head, stomp its hooves, and swish its tail. When it finally became evident to the owner that hers was a unilateral love — that her recalcitrant horse showed no signs of reform or reciprocation of her affections — she acquiesced and meekly put the horse on the market for exactly the sum that she had paid.

In a sense, that could have been a happy ending, reality triumphing over romanticism. But unfortunately, the story doesn't stop there. The woman had learned nothing about the nature or psychology of the horse from her experience. Like an unlucky lover who hopscotches from partner to partner, always convinced that the right one is just around the corner, she was certain she simply had not yet found the right horse for her. The search continued, and another Arabian was bought. But bonding worked no better the second time.

After several years of living away and losing contact with the rider, I ran into her unexpectedly at a different stable. Nothing had changed. She was visiting the stable to look for yet another horse to buy—the right one, which would somehow provide all of the emotional sustenance the others had been incapable of offering.

My guess is that, even today, this rider is still in search of the perfect equine relationship.

That's not to say that some real emotional exchange doesn't occur between horse and rider. Certainly it does every day. But the nature of the exchange is different from that between humans and other animals, with its own dynamics. The warm eagerness of a dog's wagging tail has no parallel in any behavior exhibited by members of the equine realm; nor does the sybaritic purring and rubbing of an independent cat.

© Richard Day

OPPOSITE PAGE: AN IDEAL HORSE FACILITY OFFERS GOOD, DURABLE FENCING WITH NO LOOSE OR SHARP WIRES ON WHICH AN ANIMAL COULD GET NICKED. ABOVE: TO KEEP THIS THOROUGHBRED'S COAT CLEAN OF DIRT AND SWEAT, ITS TRAINER GIVES IT A SHAMPOO AFTER A HARD WORKOUT. BUT SHAMPOOING TOO FREQUENTLY DRIES UP NATURAL OILS THAT KEEP THE HORSE'S COAT HEALTHY. THOROUGH GROOMING WITH A DANDY BRUSH FOLLOWED BY A BODY RUB WITH THE PALM OF YOUR HAND DOES WONDERS FOR BRINGING OUT THE LUSTER IN THE ANIMAL'S COAT. PAGES 38-39: THE GREATEST EMOTIONAL PAYOFF IN OWNING A HORSE COMES WHEN HOURS OF HARD WORK IN TRAINING FINALLY SINK IN—SOMETHING AS SIMPLE, PERHAPS, AS WHEN THE HORSE FINALLY SHOWS THAT AFTER WEEKS OF WORKING THROUGH TINY PUDDLES, IT HAS OVERCOME ITS FEAR OF WATER.

© FPG International

*M*r. Ed could talk, Trigger could count, and for a testament to the horse's emotional capacity, one need look no further than literature to learn of the animal's ability to have life-long love for its owner. With this portrayal of the animal at every flip of the page or flick of the television remote, no wonder the public unwittingly, but erroneously, has become convinced that horse sense rivals the workings of the human brain.

The truth is that the brain of the horse is disproportionately small in relation to its overall size. The majesty of its physical presence does not equate to a comparably majestic presence of mind. The horse can, in fact, bond to humans, but this is less a "love" response in the human understanding of the term, than it is a simple instinctive response founded on trust-building experiences.

The horse is essentially a herd animal, whose safety is best felt in numbers. For equestrians, this means that getting a horse to perform a new task — be it crossing a river on a trail ride or clearing a jump for the first time — can be facilitated by engaging in the activity with other riders, whose horses go first. The racetrack is the most dramatic example of manipulation of this herd instinct. Recognition of the herd instinct can also result in humans avoiding the development of undesirable or neurotic traits in the horse: the key simply is to make an effort to keep the horse stabled or pastured in the company of other horses, not alone.

Another factor influencing the behavior of the horse is its flight instinct. In the wild, when threatened, the horse's recourse is retreat. Domesticated horses that bolt, refuse jumps, or compulsively behave skittishly are not making a statement of defiance but of fear. Understanding this and working to alleviate the horse's fear, rather than punishing it for what is mistakenly perceived as deliberate truculence, will build the horse's trust in its rider. Once this kind of confidence has been instilled, the horse will sublimate its instinctive flight response, reacting instead to the clear aids and directions from its rider. The most readily responsive, cooperative behavior from a horse, then, isn't necessarily evidence of the animal's superior intelligence, but that of its rider — or, at least, of its rider's ability to comprehend the mind of the horse and to act accordingly.

At its best, the relationship between horse and rider is one of mutual respect, more than anything. Riders who give their horses consistent messages and operate from a rewards system of training, which includes calm but quick discipline when necessary, find a responsiveness in the horse's performance that translates as an emotional reward for the rider. In respecting the horse's integrity — understanding its fears, its herd instincts, its likes and dislikes, its tendency to try to get away with as much incorrect behavior as it possibly can — the rider provides a calm, secure atmosphere in which the horse can function at its best.

The horse accustomed to gentle but firm handling on a regular basis will give its utmost, responding to the request of its rider even when that request triggers some deep, inherent fear. At those times when the horse goes against its better instincts to honor the desire of the rider, that clear expression of animal trust can't help but act on the human heart.

A camel is a horse designed by a committee.
Anonymous

Weeks of building a relationship of trust with my Arabian gelding, Que Larque, for example, paid off the afternoon I crossed the Brazos River after days of severe flooding throughout Texas. Only recently had Que Larque and I worked through his fear of stepping into puddles (his proclivity was to jump them — no matter how large). After repetition and success, we had worked our way from puddles to the river at low tide. Now, I was asking him to cross the swollen river, with currents so swift they whisked us downstream nearly as soon as we left the dry bank. To make matters worse, I was also asking him to be the lead horse, striking a path for my friend on his borrowed horse to follow.

As we approached the water, I felt Que Larque's entire mass tremble with fear beneath me. His cautious walk froze to a halt at the river's edge. He

attempted to turn his head to retreat, and then began the in-place dance that is the Arabian's signature response to fear.

But then something happened. He heard my voice. And he felt my hand, reassuring him in long, firm strokes. Que Larque entered the water and, swimming, led us safely to the other side—several hundred yards downstream.

Hindsight informs me that the challenge I presented to Que Larque that day was unfair—even foolish. Given the unusual river conditions, Que Larque's horse sense surpassed my own. A more judicious rider would have gauged the current and opted for another day's hack. The vertigo I experienced during our crossing eloquently made the point, albeit too late to matter: we all could have drowned.

WHEN RIDING AN INEXPERIENCED HORSE THROUGH A BODY OF WATER FOR THE FIRST TIME, IT'S A GOOD IDEA TO FOLLOW A MORE VETERAN ANIMAL OR AT LEAST RIDE IN THE COMPANY OF ANOTHER. HORSES ARE HERD ANIMALS AND INSTINCTIVELY FEEL SAFER IN COMPANY.

Que Larque's exemplary physical strength in keeping his head up and swimming the river with me clutched vulnerably to his back was in itself incentive to bond; his courage to continue in the face of real danger was grounds for respect. His unquestioning trust in me, even to the point of quelling his much-justified fear, was an invitation to love.

From that experience, it would be easy to take the next leap of logic and say that, in these circumstances, a horse becomes a beloved pet like any other—an honorary member of the family.

LETTING GO

No matter how intense and poignant the bonding that occurs between horse and rider (and given the right handling of the horse, these experiences are bound to take place), the relationship is still different from any other, and it must be played according to a unique set of rules. Even after establishing such a strong bond with Que Larque, I may someday have to face the hard fact that I must part with him, as career demands intensify and travel keeps me from the stable for weeks at a time. Although to the new or potential horse owner this kind of distancing may seem callous, all business and no heart, it is a grim reality of horse ownership. Horses are too valuable, too capable of performance, too expensive to maintain, to justify hanging on to out of sheer sentimentality.

A word of warning to parents, too: should you decide to indulge your child's heart's desire and buy a horse, you may have to face wrenching that same child's heart later by selling the animal. With horses, there are no guarantees. The horse that rode well on trial, that seemed even-tempered and calm, may prove different at some later date. The animal may even be dangerous for your child—a situation that leaves you no option but to sell.

When my daughter Meagan turned four, I bought a horse for her and myself to share—a small overo paint named Brandy. The horse was fine to ride most of the time—except when she went into season. Then hormones took control, transforming her into an animal that would bolt with no provocation other than the chemical battle raging within. Meagan cried, but I eventually sold Brandy to another girl who was considerably older, and who was more capable of controlling her.

Making the decision to buy or not buy a horse is like deciding whether or not to marry: romance is fine, as long as it doesn't displace reality.

ABOVE: NOTHING IS MORE ENDEARING THAN A MARE AND FOAL, BUT IT ISN'T ALWAYS FEASIBLE TO KEEP BOTH ANIMALS FOREVER. ONE OF THE HARDEST LESSONS IN HORSEMANSHIP IS LEARNING WHEN TO LET GO, FOR WHATEVER REASON. OPPOSITE PAGE: THE SPIRITED HORSE ISN'T FOR EVERYONE. IT'S IMPORTANT TO BE HONEST ABOUT THE LEVEL OF YOUR RIDING EXPERTISE BEFORE DECIDING ON THE ANIMAL FOR YOU. ASK YOURSELF: CAN YOU HANDLE A HORSE WITH A PROCLIVITY FOR BUCKING AND REARING?

The Right Stuff: Choosing With Confidence

© Peter Beard/Visions

O! for a horse with wings!
William Shakespeare, Cymbeline II

PAGE 45: THE WILD MUSTANG IS A SCRUB HORSE THAT'S A DESCENDANT OF THE FIRST ARABIANS BROUGHT TO NORTH AMERICA BY THE SPANISH CONQUISTADORS. ABOVE: HORSES ARE LIKE RIDERS: THEY HAVE DIFFERENT LOOKS, PERSONALITIES, AND ABILITIES, AND THEREFORE, APPEAL TO DIFFERENT TYPES OF PEOPLE.

TO THINE OWN SELF BE TRUE

Like any other close relationship, the one between rider and horse involves not only a knowledge of the other party, but of self. Ideally, the process of self-discovery begins early on, in the selection stage, as you prepare to start your search for the horse that's best suited for you.

Before you can wisely choose a horse to buy, you must know yourself—your own physical type, your skills level, and what's most important to you: spirit or stability, speed or safety, docility or devil-may-care dare, beauty or old-fashioned function. Unless you take the time to know intimately these things and more, you may wake up one day to discover yourself the owner of a horse sadly unsuited to your needs and desires.

The aesthetically oriented person who cannot be happy unless surrounded by physical beauty would not be pleased with a horse of unremarkable type and color, no matter how divine the ride. On the other hand, it would be foolish for a rider whose sole interest in owning a horse is to take a good hack in the woods to invest in an Arabian with a perfect tail set, tippy ears, and dish profile; none of these physical traits affect the ride, but they do drive the price of the animal up.

After you have completed an honest assessment of self, of your needs, wants, and abilities, you are ready to make some preliminary decisions as to what kind of horse is best for you. (One of the first of these decisions will be a determination of breed—see chapter four.)

AGE

A general rule of thumb regarding equine age is "older is calmer." And that, put to practical application, means "the younger the rider, the older the horse." A young child with no riding experience should not be mounted on a green (barely broken) horse. Nor should a rider who wants to relax more than work. One year in the life of a horse is roughly equivalent to three years of human life. A two-year-old horse equates to a six-year-old child: this mount is just getting old enough to be broken to saddle and trained; it can hardly be expected to demonstrate the mellowness that comes with maturity.

A consensus in the horse community has a horse reaching real maturity at age six (although for show purposes, the age is reduced to only four). But a six-year-old horse, though well schooled by now if given proper handling, still is not the calm animal it will be in four more years. Horses are not considered aged until they reach about twelve years. And then, that term refers to full maturity, with no pejorative connotations such as senility. The average horse will live between twenty and thirty years, and most will be capable of delivering a decent, calm ride until close to the end.

For general purposes, the optimum age for a good riding horse is between about four or six, to fourteen. After fourteen, the horse still has many years of service, but its days are becoming numbered. If docility is the most important consideration, though, the greater age may be more of an attraction than a detriment.

Retirement for the horse usually occurs when it reaches its early twenties. But thanks to improved health and dietary care, not only the family pet but "professional" horses are able to extend their careers. The famous white leaping Lipizzaners of Vienna's Spanish Riding School are not forced into retirement until they prove unfit; for some, that can mean a show career for up to thirty years of age. Eight consecutive international competitions were won by the show jumper Democrat when he was campaigning for the Olympics at nineteen years of age. Silver Mint, a jumper in London, carried his young rider to a win when the horse was the ripe age of twenty-eight.

There are some age-related terms that are helpful to know when communicating with horsemen.

Foal: A horse after birth and to one year of age.
Suckling: A nursing foal.
Weanling: A foal from the time it is weaned to age one.
Filly: A female horse four years of age and under.
Colt: A male horse three years of age and under.
Mare: A female horse five years of age and older (whether or not she has been bred).
Stallion: A male horse four years of age and older.
Gelding: A castrated male horse at any age.
Green: A newly trained horse, no younger than two or three years of age.
Mature: A horse from age six to about ten or twelve years.
Aged: A horse that's fully mature, about ten or twelve years of age and older (this does not imply senility or any other negative trait).

Gender

A horse's gender affects its disposition and performance in the same manner as does age. Mare, gelding, stallion—each is different, and whether those differences translate as good or bad depends on your intent in ownership.

For an all-around riding horse, a gelding is probably the best option. A castrated stallion, a gelding has a much calmer temperament than a stallion, is easier to handle, and is far less dangerous. Likewise, a gelding tends to be more even-keeled than a mare, which can be moody with shifts in hormones. A drawback in owning a gelding, however, is that, should the animal suffer an injury that negates its ability to function as a riding horse, there is little else it can be used for, except as an object of affection (and expense).

ABOVE: THE CLICHE OF BEING PUT "OUT TO PASTURE" ORIGINATES, OF COURSE, WITH THE HORSE. HORSES ARE USUALLY RETIRED FROM THEIR ATHLETIC CAREERS IN THEIR EARLY TWENTIES, BUT SOME HAVE BEEN KNOWN TO MAINTAIN A SHOW CAREER EVEN INTO THEIR EARLY THIRTIES. BELOW: ONE OF THE ADVANTAGES IN OWNING A MARE IS THAT, IN ADDITION TO PROVIDING A GOOD RIDE OR PERFORMING IN COMPETITION, IT CAN BE BRED AND PRODUCE A FOAL. A DISADVANTAGE OF A MARE, COMPARED TO A GELDING, IS ITS MORE UNSTABLE TEMPERAMENT WHEN IN HEAT.

THE HORSE

A mare, somewhere between a gelding and a stallion in terms of docility, can, on the other hand, continue to be bred and produce foals, even if her ability in the show ring or on the trail has been impaired. Mares go into heat every twenty-one days, though, and are subject to irritability during this time. How much they are affected varies from mare to mare: they can become difficult to handle on the ground, responding adversely to grooming by attempting to kick or bite, or they can become spooked on the trail, bolting at whim.

For a riding horse, a stallion should be the last consideration. These horses function primarily for breeding. They should not be owned by amateurs, and unless they exhibit potential for show or race, they should be allowed to do nothing more than stand at stud. The intense spirit of a stallion can be alluring, but the dangers are seldom worth the gamble. Incidences of horses rearing and trampling their handlers are almost exclusively within the domain of the stallion.

Stallions are difficult to pasture, too, jumping clear of most obstacles to reach a mare in season. For the safety of other riders, they are better stabled alone. I have seldom been as frightened as the day a stallion from an adjacent pasture jumped the fence while I was riding my mare, who was in heat. The stallion meant business, charging at us with teeth bared, intent on mounting. Owners of stallions should take their responsibilities very seriously.

ABOVE: HORSES' HEIGHTS ARE MEASURED ACCORDING TO "HANDS," WITH ONE HAND EQUAL TO ABOUT FOUR INCHES (10 CM). OPPOSITE PAGE: STALLIONS SHOULD BE SEGREGATED FROM OTHER HORSES IN THE PASTURE, FOR THE SAFETY OF THE OTHER ANIMALS AND THEIR OWNERS.

Size

The measurement used to describe the height of a horse is known as a *hand*—the equivalent of four inches (10 cm). Horses are measured in hands from the bottom of their hooves to the top of their withers. The average height is 15.2 hands (62 inches or 155 cm), which should accommodate any rider of average height and weight.

Animals below 14.2 hands tall are technically classified as ponies, whether they are of a pony breed or not. Thus, a 14.1-hand Arabian or paint should actually be described as an Arabian pony or as a paint pony, not as a horse. For persons short in height, these horses are ideal mounts, for they are not so tall that they cannot be controlled effectively with the rider's hands and legs.

Rarely do saddle horses exceed seventeen hands. Any horse sixteen hands or taller is quite tall and is best ridden by a tall rider. Although the short rider on a tall horse may feel uncomfortable so far from the ground, this disproportion entails less physical discomfort than does a tall rider on a short horse—for the tall rider's legs must be unnaturally bent, folding up beneath him or her when on a short horse, and this does not produce a good riding seat or optimum performance. The general rule is that the rider should have ample "leg room" and should not be too heavy to be easily carried by the horse.

Height is often a characteristic of breed. Arabians, for example, tend to be relatively short, while Thoroughbreds are taller. Still, within each breed there is some range—though it would be rare to find a Thoroughbred under fourteen hands, or an Arabian topping out at seventeen.

Color

The color of a horse has no effect on its performance or disposition—only on the attitude of its owner. Young equestrians, especially, are prone to bedazzlement by a flashy coat. (It was not happenstance that, as a teenager, my first horse was a golden palomino.)

When shopping for a horse, or when conducting any intelligent conversation with horse folks, it helps to have a working knowledge of the vocabulary. The colors of the horse are not as self-evident as they might seem, but bear some definition.

Albino: This coat is white and the horse's eyes are blue.

Appaloosa: Commonly thought of as spotted horses, Appaloosas (which have their own breed registry) vary greatly in color. Typically, they are characterized by a white area on the hips and loin, which is interspersed with small dark spots.

Bay: The coat color ranges from golden tan to a rich mahogany. But the mane, tail, and lower legs must always be black for the horse to truly be a bay.

Black: Not only must the coat itself be pure black, but also the flank and muzzle.

Brown: The coat color can be brown or black, but the hair around the muzzle or flank must be brown.

Buckskin: The coat color resembles that of a palomino, ranging from a tan to a dull brown, but it is accentuated by a black mane, tail, and lower legs, and a black stripe across the top of the back.

Chestnut: This coat color ranges from bright copper to sorrel (a light red), on to a deep liver. The mane and tail must be either the same color as the coat or a lighter color; they cannot be darker.

Dun: The dun's coat is a gray-tinged yellow, while the mane, tail, and lower legs, plus the dorsal (back) stripe, are black.

Gray: Gray horses are born black, bay, or chestnut, then fade through successive stages of gray, often becoming dappled. They can be distinguished as gray horses at birth by scattered gray hairs around the eyes.

Palomino: The coat color is golden. Mane and tail are white or silver.

Pinto: Pintos have large spots and are subcategorized into two divisions: overo, meaning pintos with a dark coat and large white spots; and tobiano, meaning pintos with a white coat and large dark spots.

Roan: This coat can be any fairly dark color, as long as the base color is intermixed with white hairs throughout. A blue roan refers to a black base coat mixed with white; a strawberry roan describes a chestnut coat that is mixed with white.

ABOVE: DESPITE THE MYTH THAT BROWN HORSES ARE DEPENDABLE AND STEADY, A HORSE'S COLORATION HAS NO EFFECT ON ITS TEMPERAMENT. OPPOSITE PAGE, TOP: THE APPALOOSA'S COAT CAN HAVE ONE OF SIX MAIN PATTERNS; HOWEVER, EACH HORSE'S COLORATION IS UNIQUE IN ITS OWN WAY. OPPOSITE PAGE, BOTTOM: PALOMINOS ARE HORSES WHOSE COATS ARE A GOLDEN COLOR, WITH MANES AND TAILS OF WHITE OR SILVER. BREEDING TWO PALOMINOS DOES NOT AUTOMATICALLY ENSURE PRODUCING A FOAL THAT IS PALOMINO; RATHER, LUCK IS REQUIRED. PALOMINOS, THEN, ARE NOT A BREED OF HORSE BUT A COLOR. HOWEVER, THERE IS A PALOMINO REGISTRY TO WHICH THEY CAN BELONG.

THE RIGHT STUFF: CHOOSING WITH CONFIDENCE

THE HORSE

MARKINGS

In addition to color, the horse's physical appearance is described by markings on its head and legs.

Bald face: A marking that colors the entire face white.

Blaze: A white marking that begins at the forehead and extends to cover the nose.

Snip: A white facial mark between the nostrils.

Sock: White on the leg above the fetlock to no farther than halfway up the canon bone.

Star: A white facial mark on the forehead.

Stocking: White on the leg from above the fetlock and continuing farther than halfway up the canon bone.

Strip: A narrow white mark that descends down the horse's head.

OPPOSITE PAGE: COMMON-SENSE, DESCRIPTIVE TERMS ARE USED TO INDICATE THE COLORS OF THE PARTS OF A HORSE. A SOCK, FOR EXAMPLE, REFERS TO THE WHITE ON THE LEG FROM THE FETLOCK TO NO HIGHER THAN HALFWAY UP THE CANON BONE. A STOCKING IS WHITE HAIR THAT EXTENDS HIGHER. ABOVE: THIS HORSE'S HEAD IS DISTINGUISHED BY A BLAZE—A VERTICAL WHITE BAND THAT BEGINS AT THE FOREHEAD AND EXTENDS OVER THE NOSE. LEFT: A STAR AND A STRIP ORNAMENT THIS HORSE'S HEAD.

CONFORMATION

Before buying a horse, it only makes sense to acquire as much equine knowledge as possible, for far fewer intelligent decisions are regretted than those made out of ignorance. The soundness of your horse — its overall health, fitness, and ability to perform the tasks requested — need not be guesswork or a shadowy subject for future revelation. Soundness is largely contingent on conformation: the basic build of the horse. The trained eye can anticipate potential unsoundness in a horse by spotting areas of weakness or aberrations in its physique — in the visual paradigm of good conformation. But to do this, it is essential first to be grounded in how the animal ideally should look. Doing your homework on the anatomy of the horse will pay off in your selection of a much better mount.

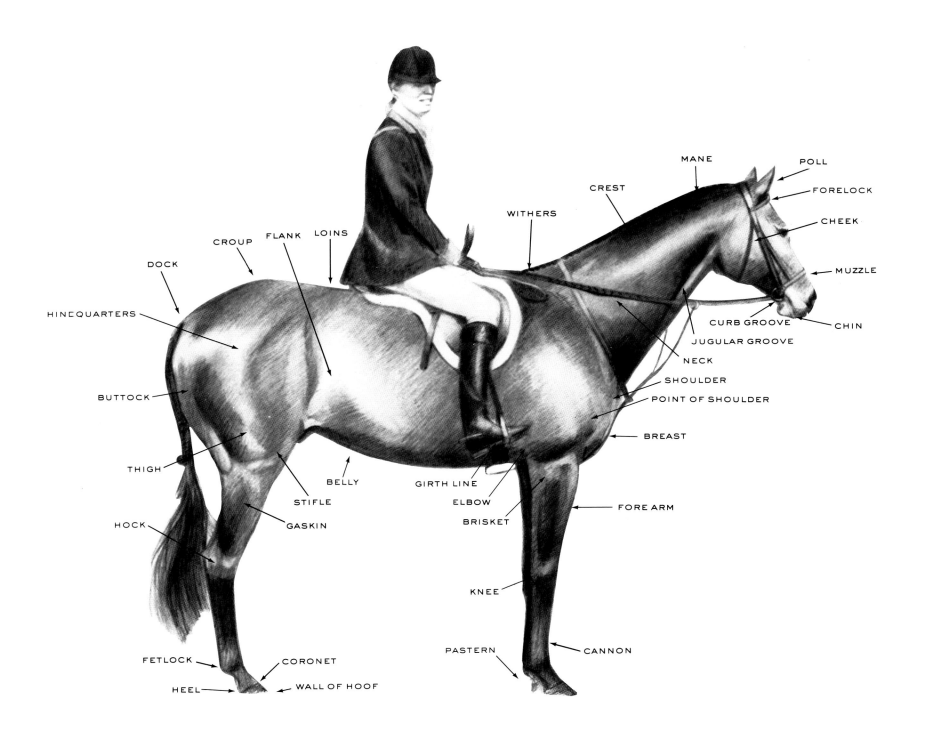

THE POINTS OF THE HORSE: A FAMILIARITY WITH THE HORSE'S ANATOMY IS A FUNDAMENTAL PART OF HORSEMANSHIP.

MANE

POLL

CREST

FORELOCK

WITHERS

CHEEK

FLANK   LOINS

CROUP

MUZZLE

DOCK

CURB GROOVE

CHIN

HINEQUARTERS

JUGULAR GROOVE

NECK

SHOULDER

BUTTOCK

POINT OF SHOULDER

BREAST

THIGH

BELLY

GIRTH LINE

STIFLE

ELBOW

FORE ARM

GASKIN

BRISKET

HOCK

KNEE

PASTERN

CANNON

FETLOCK

CORONET

HEEL

WALL OF HOOF

by Chris Cancelli

Heads or Tails

A common mistake made by neophytes in sizing up a horse is to begin with the head, then move on, as the eye naturally travels, to inspect the shoulders, chest, and eventually the tail. Many an inferior animal has been bought based on nothing more than the allure of a pretty head.

The better way to approach judging conformation—the way of the seasoned equestrian—is to get an overall picture of the horse in one broad sweep of a look. That is, take in visually as much as you possibly can of the animal. Check to see if anything stands out as unusual. Are there any breaks in symmetry? Any discordance in an otherwise harmonious image? Think of it as a version of the children's game, "what's wrong with this picture?" If the horse's back seems too long, then probably it is—and that's a flaw in conformation that best be acknowledged, as it is likely to result in weakness.

After looking at the big picture, try dividing the horse into halves with imaginary lines to check for symmetry among the parts. Do this from the front, from the side, and from the rear. On a horse with good conformation, the rear view should show you that the horse's hind feet are closer together than the front feet, and that the point of the hock and the thighs touch the same imaginary vertical line. Because the legs and feet are the most important features of the horse, if this comprehensive scan of them reveals a problem, you need not continue with your scrutiny.

If all seems in order thus far, it's time to do a more intensive examination of the legs. Each leg must support approximately three hundred pounds (480 kg) of bulk. If the legs are weak, the horse is virtually useless. Therefore, it's imperative to scrutinize this part of the animal's anatomy with great care.

The front legs support more weight than the back legs—nearly two-thirds of the horse's total weight—so they demand the closest look. First, check from the front to see if the legs drop straight or if they taper. If they taper, becoming more narrow at the feet than at the chest, this means the feet are likely to interfere with each other as the horse moves through the gaits.

The forearms should be long, as this length correlates directly to the horse's stride. Long forearms result in a long, smooth stride. Below the forearms are the knees—a common site of weakness. Generally, the knees should be square in appearance, flat, not puffy, and wide, instead of narrow. Just as the muscles around the knees should not puff, nor should they constrict. This fault is known as tied-in and results in the animal having difficulty being flexible and free in its stride. Tied-in is an inherited disorder and cannot be corrected. A tendon that curves outward is considered bowed—a sign of damage through overwork, which cannot be remedied.

Perhaps the most important part of the leg to examine is farther down, at the pastern. This is the shock absorber of the horse, the portion of the body under constant wear. If not properly formed to begin with, the pastern will break down and the horse will not be sound. Pasterns ideally take about a forty-five-degree angle and are fairly long. This ensures a smooth ride without too much pressure on the pastern. A straight, short pastern means a choppy ride, because the absorp-

SUPRASPINATUS

INFRASPINATUS

TRICEPS

BICEPS BRACHIL

LATERAL CARPAL FLEXOR

RADIAL CARPAL EXTENSOR

COMMON DIGITAL EXTENSOR

DEEP DIGITAL FLEXOR

LATERAL DIGITAL EXTENSOR

ANNULAR LIGAMENTS

TENDON OF DEEP DIGITAL FLEXOR

Illustration by Linda Krause

THE MUSCLES OF A HORSE'S LEG. MORE THAN ANY OTHER PART OF THE HORSE'S ANATOMY, THE LEG IS CRITICAL TO SOUNDNESS—A FACT NOT HARD TO UNDERSTAND, GIVEN THAT THE SLENDER LEGS SUPPORT ABOUT A HALF-TON (.45 T) OF WEIGHT.

tion of shock is minimal. It also means potential damage to other muscles in the leg of the horse, as a result of the impact of the stride not being properly cushioned. Straight pasterns also cause the weight of the animal to be distributed over the navicular bone, the smallest bone in the hoof, which is often the site of disabling lameness. At the opposite extreme, a pastern that slopes too much, more than forty-five degrees, means that the ride will be smooth, but the pastern will be weak and may eventually result in unsoundness.

THE SKELETAL STRUCTURE OF THE HORSE.

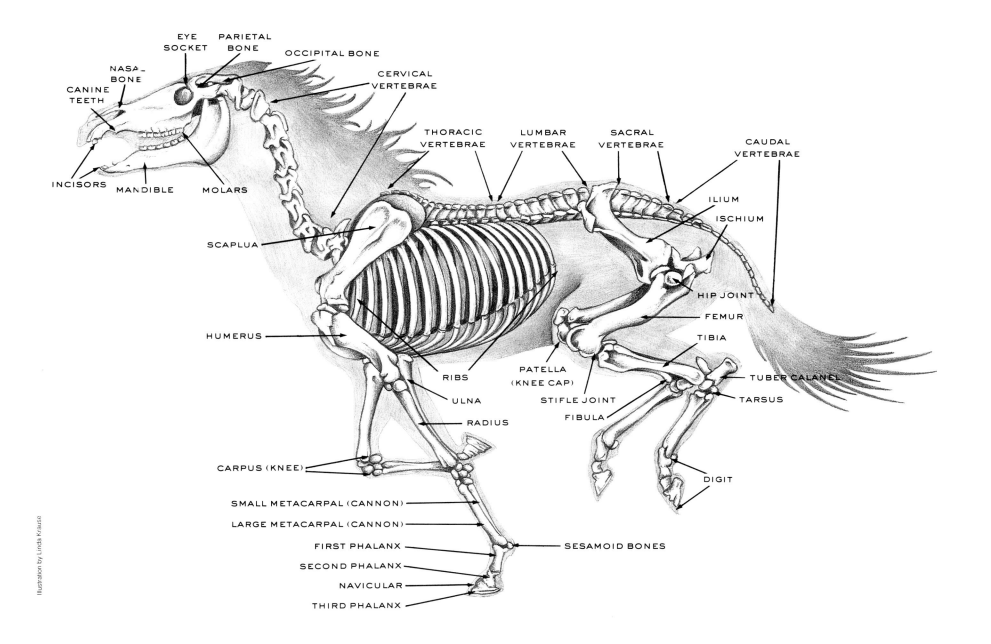

Illustration by Linda Krause

Horses are athletes, and as such, they are entirely dependent on the soundness and strength of their bodies for a successful performance.

© Daniel E. Dempster/Dembinsky Photo Associates

THE HORSE

The horse's feet should be proportionate in size to the rest of the body. Feet that are too small mean that the horse will have trouble supporting its own weight and may become unsound; feet that are too large mean that the horse will be clumsy and won't give you a pleasurable ride. Forefeet should be round and hind feet oval. Forefeet should point straight ahead, not in or out.

As the extension of the pastern, the hoof itself should follow a forty-five-degree angle. It should be wide and full at the heel, as well as at the toe. Its outer horn should be hard and free of ridges and cracks. The frog—rubbery, sensitive tissue in the center of the underside of the hoof—should extend down in a V-shape to grip the ground in order to help prevent slipping and act as a shock absorber.

An examination of the back legs is basically identical to that of the front legs, but with some additional considerations. The hindquarters, as the propelling force, should be muscled up, especially in the gaskin, thigh, and stifle. The thigh muscles should be pronounced both on the inside and outside, and they should carry on down into the gaskin. When muscling is absent at the gaskin, the horse is considered "cat-hammed."

The hocks are important in providing impulsion and in reducing the impact of the hooves when the horse is taking strides. Accordingly, they should be well defined with sharply pronounced bones. Viewed from the rear, they should point as straight ahead as possible. If they turn in, the horse is considered "cow hocked"; if they turn out, it is "bowlegged" or "bandy legged." Bandy legs are especially bad, putting severe stress on the hocks and causing them to rotate with each movement of the horse.

After this thorough investigation of the legs and feet, next study the animal's top line, from the poll (at the head) to the root of the tail. This line should be fairly straight among breeds such as saddlebreds and Arabians, just as the line on the underside of the horse in general should also be horizontal. More slope in the hindquarters is favored in some breeds. The back should not be too low or the horse is considered swaybacked—a common sign of old age. The opposite formation, a convex or arched back, is rare and is a source of real problems with extension and flexion of the horse's legs. On all saddle horses, the withers, the points at which the shoulder muscles attach to the spine, should always be higher than the hindquarters, and the back should be short, while the underline is long. The rib cage should curve outward, as opposed to laying flat.

The head should be balanced, neither too big nor too small for the neck. The neck ideally will be long and flexible with good muscle tone; from the back it will appear thick and solid, while from the side it will assume a more graceful, slender look. The neck is more than an aesthetic concern. It actually has an impact on how the horse moves. The ride of a horse with a short, thick neck will be less smooth than that of a horse with a longer, slimmer neck—for the neck is used in balancing the animal. A short, thick neck results in a short, choppy gait. A neck that is too long, on the other hand, is also not desirable. This neck type will result in the horse tiring easily. The worst two conformations of the neck are the swan neck, which is exaggeratedly arched, and the ewe neck, which has the opposite problem of looking as if it were upside down.

THIS STUDY FOR THE SFORZA MONUMENT (C. 1490) BY LEONARDO DA VINCI SHOWS THE ARTIST'S UNDERSTANDING OF THE HORSE'S CONFORMATION.

The horse's shoulders ideally should be long, following about a forty-five-degree angle. The withers are not important to the horse in terms of soundness, but they do make a difference to the comfort of the rider. Withers keep the saddle on. A horse without withers requires the rider to dismount constantly and tighten the girth to avoid slipping off the saddle.

Chests vary among breeds (quarter horses are known for their wide barrel chests), but basically they should be wide, deep at the girth, to provide maximum room for lung and heart development and attendant stamina. Horses without a deep girth (this trait must be determined by looking at the animal from the side) always lack stamina. To get a better idea of how the girth should look, follow this yardstick: the circumference of the girth should never be less than the horse's height. If the girth exceeds the horse's height by ten inches (25 cm), that is considered very good. The girth's shape should be oval, not round.

In the loin region, the horse should be broad and heavily muscled. It is a plus if the loin is short, for this means maximum strength and weight-carrying capability. The flank, just beneath the loin, should be deep; otherwise, the horse is considered "wasp waisted"—a flaw.

The last part of the top line, the croup, refers to the area between the hips and buttocks. The croup should not slope too greatly downward (horses with

© Bob Pool/Tom Stack & Associates

a steep croup are known as "goose rumped") because this places the hind legs too far under the body and limits the horse's ability to extend its gaits. The croup should be long, not short, to ensure power and length of stride.

MAGIC IN THE MOTION

Chances are good that, if the horse you are considering has excellent conformation, it also will have outstanding action. But it's important to verify this on the ground, as well as in the saddle. (In the saddle, it's easy to become preoccupied with how quickly and how well the horse responds to your cues. The well-schooled horse may have great alacrity in responding to your aids, but its stride may not be as smooth as it should be. An inspection from the ground can help you check this important point.)

Watch another rider on the horse, or watch the horse being lounged. Does it have free, even, elastic strides? Are the animal's legs moving forward in a straight line, with no deviation to either side? Check from both the front

THE HORSE'S FASTEST NATURAL GAIT IS THE GALLOP, A FOUR-BEAT GAIT IN WHICH EACH HOOF STRIKES THE GROUND INDIVIDUALLY.

and back to be sure. Now try out the horse in the saddle. Take the animal through the various gaits:

Walk: A slow four-beat gait with each foot lifting and striking the ground individually.

Trot: A clipped, diagonal two-beat gait with the opposite pairs of front and hind feet lifting and striking the ground at the same time.

Canter: A calm, collected three-beat gait with a front leg striking first, then a hind leg and the other front leg striking together, followed by the other hind leg pushing off and starting the whole process again. (Technically, the hind leg is the first to set this gait in action, but because judging in the show ring is based on correct leads—a canter to the right should "lead" with the right front leg, a canter to the left should lead with the left front leg—it is convenient to describe the gait as beginning with the front leg.)

WALK

TROT

CANTER

GALLOP

Illustration by Linda Krause

THE HORSE

Gallop: A faster four-beat gait with much extension, the hind legs far behind the body propel the horse forward and the front legs extended forward collect the motion and prepare to begin again.

Additional gaits that may or may not apply to your horse include:

Running walk: A slow four-beat gait that's a little quicker than a regular walk. It is achieved by the hind foot overstepping the front foot to produce the sensation of gliding. The horse often nods in time with the beat. This gait is easy on the horse and is a joy for the rider.

Pace: A fast two-beat, lateral gait with the same-side fore and hind legs moving together as a pair. This gait is used only by harness racers on a smooth track.

Stepping or slow pace: The slow four-beat gait is the specialty of the five-gaited show horse. Unlike the regular pace, this gait doesn't have same-side legs moving forward precisely together; thus it eliminates the uncomfortable rolling action of the regular pace. Each hoof strikes separately, although the pairs of legs appear to be moving together.

Fox trot: This is another special gait sometimes used as the slow gait of five-gaited horses. It is a broken trot in which the hind foot strikes the ground a second or so before its paired diagonal front foot strikes. The horse nods its head in time with the beat.

Rack: A fast, unnatural four-beat gait that is easy on the rider and hard on the horse. A specialty of the saddlebred, this gait makes for a brilliant spectacle at the horse's expense.

© Norvia Behling

TEMPERAMENT

A horse with perfect conformation and action but an undesirable personality clearly isn't the horse for you. Just like people, horses have individual differences in disposition. It is a bit easier than with people, however, to make a determination of a horse's temperament, thanks to some basic traits associated with breed (see chapter 4).

While individuals will vary on how spirited or how docile a horse they want, overall most riders prefer their mount to be bold and confident, so as not to shy or refuse at the least provocation, and at the same time to be passive enough to be manageable. The pleasure rider doesn't need a horse so high-strung that it bolts on the trail, destroying the peace of the ride. The show-ring rider, on the other hand, may appreciate the flash and high energy of the spirited animal, even when it means difficulty in maintaining control.

© Christopher Bain

TOP: AS WITH ANY RELATIONSHIP, THE ONE BE-TWEEN HORSE AND HUMAN DEMANDS COMPATIBLE PERSONALITIES. WHILE CHILDREN HAVE A NATURAL AFFECTION FOR YOUNG HORSES, THEY ARE MORE WISELY PAIRED WITH AN OLDER HORSE WHEN IT'S TIME FOR RIDING. CHILDREN LACK THE EXPERIENCE TO MANAGE THE UNPREDICTA-BILITY OF A VERY YOUNG HORSE. BOTTOM: FOR MOST PLEASURE RIDERS, THE IDEAL HORSE IS ONE THAT HAS A CALM, WILLING DISPOSITION.

CHAPTER FOUR

BREEDS

*B*oot, saddle, to horse, and away!
Robert Browning, Boot and Saddle

Equestrians are like proud parents: ask any rider which breed of horse is best, and no doubt he or she will glibly tell you—quite coincidentally, of course, his or her own. Selecting a breed is one of the most important decisions facing the prospective horse owner, for horses vary in temperament, ability, and appearance according to breed. To avoid undue confusion, first determine what it is you expect from your animal.

Are you interested in a pleasure horse only, a reliable, gentle animal for pleasant hacking on a sunny weekend afternoon? Or are you interested in competing with your horse in the show ring and, if so, in which classes? The horse that excels as a hunter-jumper, or in dressage, may not be the one that will serve you best in western pleasure or trail classes. Before listening to the various sales pitches of admittedly biased horse persons, you must be sure to have your needs and expectations clearly identified.

If your goal in owning a horse is noncompetitive, strictly limited to pleasure riding, you may want to circumvent the whole issue of selecting a breed, at least temporarily, until you first decide if perhaps a grade horse can satisfy your needs. Grade horses are those whose sire and dam were not purebreds and which accordingly, are not registered with a purebred society. Grade horses cost less than purebreds as a rule, unless they are highly schooled and proven victors in competition. In appearance, the grade horse may lack some of the chrome or flash associated with many breeds, as well as, perhaps, the capability to perform more specialized skills. If pedigree isn't an issue for you in horses, however, you may find a grade horse to be the most logical choice. If the grade horse you find is good, its not being a purebred actually may be more of an advantage than a disadvantage to you: many purebreds have high-strung, nervous dispositions due to genetics, while a good grade horse, in general, tends to be calmer. The purebred's volatile temperament is a quality that can be worked to the rider's favor in competition, manifested as courage and dramatic presence, but it does not translate as well on a leisurely ride in the park or woods.

SINCE THE ANCIENT GREEKS FIRST SAW THE ARABIAN AND WERE INSPIRED TO ADD WINGS AND IMMORTALIZE IT AS PEGASUS IN THEIR MYTHOLOGY, THE ARABIAN HAS CAPTIVATED HUMANS WITH ITS BEAUTY AND GRACE.

BREEDS MOST POPULAR IN NORTH AMERICA

Arabian

In a consideration of horse breeds, a logical starting point is the Arabian, the oldest and most influential of all purebreds.

To the prospective horse owner, the Arabian's distinctive physical beauty is its most noticeable feature. But in terms of its contributions to the horse population, the Arabian is most valuable for its strong gene pool. The Arabian has transmitted stamina, intelligence, and hereditary soundness to all of the world's established warm-blood breeds—that is, they were all either originally founded with Arab blood in their lineage, or, at some point in their history, the stock was improved by an introduction of Arab blood. Arab blood has also been introduced to and had an influence on many of the heavy cold-blood breeds of northwestern Europe.

One of Britain's most well-known champions of the Arabian, the late Lady Wentworth, who was the author of *The Authentic Arabian*, waxed eloquent regarding the Arab influence: "The Arab is the oldest blood stock of all. It is a Tap Root, not a derivation from anything else at all. It has the gift, possessed alone by true root stock, of absolute dominance in breeding and unrivalled power of impressing its own character on any other breed with irresistible force. The Arab is the chief and noblest origin of our national racehorse, of the best breeds of North Africa, and of light breeds all over the world."

Valuable as her contributions to our knowledge of Arabians remain, Lady Wentworth was swept away by her passion for the Arab at times, creating myth instead of passing along fact. She boldly asserted that the Arab was an established breed in 5000 B.C., "having its origin solely in the Arabian peninsula, where a separate race of wild horse having no connection with any other strain once lived and was domesticated." In truth, it is impossible to affix the Arab's genesis to a specific date—or to establish its existence by as early as 5000 B.C. It is known that the Arab was an established breed in Egypt by 1300 B.C. however, based on the horse's replication in statuary from that period. The Arab was probably around even earlier, too. A statue of a ridden horse from Egypt about 2000 B.C. bears

ABOVE: IT IS GENERALLY AGREED UPON THAT THE ARABIAN HEAD IS SINGULARLY BEAUTIFUL AMONG BREEDS. BELOW: THE ARAB'S NATURALLY HIGH TAIL SET AND ARCHED NECK CONTRIBUTE TO ITS DISTINCTIVE ELEGANCE.

© Popperfoto/Langrish

THE OLDEST AND MOST INFLUENTIAL OF ALL HORSE BREEDS, THE ARABIAN IS APPRECIATED NOT ONLY FOR ITS INHERENT QUALITIES, BUT ALSO FOR ITS ROLE IN PRODUCING OTHER BREEDS OR IMPROVING THEIR BLOODLINES.

a close resemblance to the Arabian, which implies that not only would the Arab have been an established breed by that time, but that it had been around long enough to have been domesticated by humans.

As the major contributor to the founding stock of the Thoroughbred, the Arab holds its greatest achievement. The most beautiful of all of Britain's ponies, the Welsh, also clearly shows its Arab heritage, appearing almost like a miniature Arab with its wide-set eyes and graceful dished profile.

© Popperfoto/Langrish

The great French cold-blood breed, the Percheron, originated as a cross between Arabian and Norman horses. The French Normandy is also an Arab descendant by way of the English Norfolk trotter, Young Rattler, which descended from the Godolphin Arabian. Among outstanding American breeds, the Arab, as the foundation stock of the Thoroughbred, has influenced such breeds as the standardbred (through the Thoroughbred, Messenger), and the flashy five-gaited American saddle horse.

ONE OF THE BREEDS DERIVED FROM ARABIAN BLOOD IS THE FRENCH PERCHERON, A CROSS BETWEEN ARABIAN AND NORMAN HORSES.

© Popperfoto/Langrish

The French Normandy is another descendant of the Arab. Its bloodline, through the English Norfolk trotter, Young Rattler, traces to the Godolphin Arabian.

Arabians are compact in size, ranging in height from about 14.2 to 15.2 hands. Their short heads are wide at the forehead, with an upward-curved dished profile that terminates in a narrow muzzle, giving the head its characteristic delicate elegance. Arabian ears are long and tippy. Eyes are enormous and soulful. All of these features put together have resulted in the general agreement that the Arabian head is the most refined and beautiful of all breeds.

The Arabian's head is supported by a long, arched neck, which is visually balanced by a long, high-set, and arched tail, for an aristocratic appearance. Arabians have fine, luxuriantly silky coats and a slim though athletic body.

Arabs make excellent all-around horses. They are capable of accomplishing almost any demand asked of them, though perhaps not quite as well as other purebreds bred specifically for certain specialized tasks. Their compact bodies give them incredible endurance, resulting in excellent records for the breed in endurance rides. They are good under both English and western saddle, both in the show ring and on the trail. Their small height does not make them top competitors for hunting or racing, although the all-Arab race has come into its own as a sport in recent years.

Arabians, after millennia of living alongside their Bedouin owners' tents, have an inbred sociability toward people. Though they can exhibit nervousness and spirit that might not make them the best choice for a beginner, Arabians' courage, willingness, and responsiveness to humans make them desirable mounts.

Thoroughbred

One of the most specialized breeds is the Thoroughbred. This descendant of the Arabian is in many respects the Arab's opposite: the Thoroughbred is tall and long-bodied for an overall rangy look, and it has a long, straight head that is stately but lacks the Arab's chiseled refinement and fine tapering at the muzzle. The progenitor of this horse—fastest in the world as a result of selective breeding—was actually not a single Arabian but three different Eastern stallions: the Byerley Turk, Darley Arab, and Godolphin Arab. These three horses were imported to Britain in the late seventeenth and early eighteenth centuries. It was their descendants—Herod, Eclipse, and Matchem—that served as foundation stock for the Thoroughbred.

The Thoroughbred averages sixteen hands tall, usually ranging from about 14.2 to 17.2 hands. Its height, coupled with the right conformation—a graceful neck, sloped shoulders, a deep body, short back, and powerful hindquarters—are responsible for making the Thoroughbred formidably fast. Thus, it is the premier racehorse, capable of covering a mile (1.6 km) at about forty miles (62 km) per hour. It has the distinction of being the only breed each year to have its individual horses singled out, just like any human athlete, to receive sports coverage during the famed, high-stakes Triple Crown. Just as baseball players are immortalized among fans for their RBIs and ERAs, superstar Thoroughbreds such as Seattle Slew have their outstanding records cited throughout the generations—a legitimate part of sports trivia.

ABOVE: ONE OF THE WORLD'S GREAT ATHLETES, THE THOROUGHBRED IS A VERSATILE PERFORMER, EXCELLING IN JUMPING AND OTHER EQUESTRIAN SPORTS. BELOW: A FAVORITE OF BLUE BLOOD AND BLUE COLLAR ALIKE, THOROUGHBRED RACING HAS IMPLANTED THE THOROUGHBRED BREED IN THE HEARTS OF TRACK FANS FOREVER.

© Richard Day

A LONG, LANKY BREED WITH STREAMLINED MUSCLES AND POWER, THE THOROUGHBRED IS A HIGH ACHIEVER THAT OFTEN HAS A HIGH-STRUNG DISPOSITION TO MATCH.

Thoroughbreds are fleetest, in Kentucky.
James Hilary Mulligan, In Kentucky

But the Thoroughbred isn't just prized for its feats on the track. This stellar athlete is a natural at most any event for which it has trained. Its strength and length make it a fine hunter-jumper. To some observers, it seems odd that the lean, sleek Thoroughbred possesses the raw strength required for jumping. It simply looks too thin, which seems to suggest an attendant fragility or lack of powerfulness. In truth, the Thoroughbred has dense, hard bones capable of undergoing the severely strenuous activity of show jumping and eventing.

For the novice rider, the Thoroughbred, as a rule (to which, certainly, there are exceptions), is not the best mount. Its high-strung, volatile nature requires the steady confidence and skill that only comes with experience in the saddle. But among a large percentage of veteran equestrians, including many who have no interest in competitive riding, the Thoroughbred is the first choice among the breeds—an animal which, when matched with a competent handler, assures a challenging and rewarding equine experience.

Quarter Horse

Among devotees of English equitation, the Thoroughbred is often the preferred mount, but in sheer number, the American quarter horse is the most popular of all breeds. The quarter horse registry is the largest in the world, approaching three million recorded purebreds. This quantity becomes especially significant when it is realized that the registry wasn't founded until 1941. Three factors account for the burgeoning popularity of the breed: its excellence in western riding events and its association with the Old West; its calm, docile temperament and easy manageability; and a versatility that enables it to engage reasonably well in a wide range of equestrian sports.

THE QUARTER HORSE'S NAME DERIVES FROM ITS SPECIAL ABILITY TO CLEAR SHORT DISTANCES (COLONISTS USED THE QUARTER HORSE TO RACE A QUARTER-MILE) AT FAST SPEEDS.

The quarter horse actually originated in the eastern United States, not the West, as a cross between the Arabians and Barbs of the Spanish explorers and the Thoroughbreds and Thoroughbred crosses of the English. Native Americans stole the horses brought to the New World by the Spanish in the sixteenth century, and these horses were then crossed by the English colonists in Virginia with their mounts in the seventeenth and eighteenth centuries.

The horse that developed from this cross combined the compact size, hardiness, and stamina of the Spanish Arabs and Barbs with the speed—albeit for short distances only—of the Thoroughbred. Because of its small size and quick turning ability, the quarter horse became adept at working cattle, turning with agility at breakneck speed after uncooperative bovine. This feature became inbred, and soon the quarter horse was instinctively oriented for cutting cattle. The horse, with its ranching activity and open-range grazing, was destined to become an inherent, vital part of the westward expansion of America. The horse's agility and speed in roping resulted in the development of the American rodeo, in which the quarter horse's performance at roping, cutting, and related activities is valued for pleasure only.

With its western orientation, the quarter horse is excellent for trail riding and western classes in the show ring. It can be used for polo (its cutting-horse, turn-on-a-dime agility being a real asset), show jumping, endurance riding, dressage, and English equitation, as well.

Early in its history, the breed was discovered to have vast speed and strength to carry it in short-distance racing—particularly the quarter-mile (400 m)—hence, the breed's name. America's British settlers, in fact, were first to put the horse to this use. With no formal racetracks, they created clearings of a relatively short distance wherever they could. Over time, the distance was standardized to a quarter of a mile. With its muscular, compact body, the breed provides considerable excitement for spectators with its amazing sprinting skill.

In height, the mature quarter horse averages from fourteen to sixteen hands. Its head is relatively short and broad, with full nostrils, medium ears, and a wide jaw indicative of strength. The breed's shoulders are muscular and its body is broad at the chest, affording ample room for heart and lungs to perform efficiently, thus giving the breed hardy stamina. The back is short—shorter than the animal's underline, and the barrel is deep, with a wide rib cage.

© Sally Klein

American Saddlebred

For the aficionado of the show ring and the lover of pyrotechnics, the American saddlebred, or saddle horse is no stranger. The very raison d'être of this breed is flashy performance, not mundane, utilitarian function. For the beginning equestrian or the potential horse owner wanting only a pleasure mount, the saddlebred is probably too esoteric to be the right choice. Its brilliant, animated gaits and artifically controlled high tail set have little value on the trail. The saddlebred is sensitive and high-strung, but its disposition nonetheless is gentle.

Standing from fifteen to sixteen hands high, these animals fall into two categories: the three-gaited and five-gaited saddlebreds. Three-gaited saddlebreds are shown at the walk, trot, and canter, and hence, are sometimes called "walk-trots."

Five-gaited horses perform two additional gaits, the slow gait and the rack, both of which are artificial, not performed naturally by the horse but as a result of arduous schooling. Not all saddlebreds can easily learn these two artificial gaits, thus rendering the five-gaited horse an especially rarefied animal. The slow gait is performed in an exaggerated, slow-motion, restrained style and is a high-stepping, highly collected four-beat gait. The most demanding of the two artificial gaits is the rack—a breathtakingly fast version of the slow gait, and one that is strenuous for the horse to perform. At this pace, some saddlebreds have been able to cover a mile (1.6 km) in just two minutes, nineteen seconds.

In addition to the special schooling required for the saddlebred's artificial gaits, its regular gaits also are given extra flash through artificial techniques. The breed's exuberant, high-stepping leg action is enhanced by the use of uncomfortably heavy shoes on the animals' feet, which are allowed to grow exceptionally long. Also, strictly for appearance, the horses' tails are artificially manipulated to achieve the dramatic high set. Although an emerging public consciousness of animal-rights issues may change this, it has been commonplace to nick the depressor muscles of the dock (a practice illegal in Britain for some time) to produce a high carriage. Then, the tail is set in an unnaturally high position with a tail set or brace during the time that the horse spends in its stall. To ensure that the animal doesn't lower its tail in the show ring, the practice has been to insert an irritant such as ginger in the horse's rectum.

Each of the three basic gaits of the saddlebred is a visual delight in itself: the springy four-beat walk, the high-action and spirited two-beat trot, and the extremely collected, slow, rhythmic canter. The canter is so slow and lulling, with such minimal forward motion, that it appears almost like rocking in place.

Thanks to distinctly different approaches in grooming, the three-gaited and five-gaited saddlebreds are easily distinguishable. The three-gaited's mane and tail are either roached (completely shaved) or clipped. Five-gaited saddlebreds are left with a full-flowing mane and tail.

The saddlebred originated in the southern United States in the nineteenth century as a comfortable, showy mount for plantation owners to ride while surveying the goings-on of their huge estates. The saddlebred satisfied the requirement of an aristocratic appearance so important to the landed gentry's image, and it

ABOVE: THE SADDLEBRED STANDS FROM FIFTEEN TO SIXTEEN HANDS HIGH AND HAS A STRAIGHT BUT ELEGANT HEAD WITH A SCULPTURAL PROFILE. ITS REAL CHARM, HOWEVER, CAN ONLY BE REVEALED IN MOTION. OPPOSITE PAGE: WITH THE WORLD'S LARGEST REGISTRY, THE AMERICAN QUARTER HORSE IS THE MOST POPULAR OF ALL BREEDS. A COMPACT, MUSCULAR HORSE WITH A DEEP BARREL CHEST, THE QUARTER HORSE IS NOTED FOR ITS STAMINA AND FAST TURNING ABILITY.

also offered the stamina and comfort necessary for a long day in the saddle. The breed's emergence was particularly strong in Kentucky and, in fact, the saddlebred at one time was known as the Kentucky saddler. Kentucky breeders developed the saddlebred by crossing Narragansett and Canadian pacers with Thoroughbreds, Arabians, and Morgans. The official foundation sire was the Canadian pacer stallion, Denmark. Another important sire in the saddlebred's lineage was the Canadian pacer, Tom Hall. Messenger, the Thoroughbred critical in the development of the standardbred, was also an important contributor to the saddlebred bloodline.

The medium-tall horse is usually black, bay brown, or chestnut, often with white markings. It has a straight but refined head for a sculptural profile, with small, close-set ears, large eyes and nostrils, and a fine muzzle. Its neck and shoulders are long and muscular, set off by prominent withers that define a short, straight, broad back.

ONE OF THE FLASHIEST OF ALL BREEDS, WITH ITS EXUBERANT, HIGH-STEPPING ACTION, THE AMERICAN SADDLEBRED IS CLASSIFIED AS EITHER A THREE- OR FIVE-GAITED HORSE. BOTH TYPES HAVE THEIR OWN UNIQUE GAITS.

American Standardbred

Just as the Thoroughbred was bred specifically for racing, the standardbred was developed solely to be a trotting and pacing horse. It is not a riding horse, even today. Its name, in fact, derives from its ability to trot or pace a certain distance in a "standard" time—a requirement of its registry that was enacted in 1879. Today, however, any progeny of registered standardbreds can be registered without having to fulfill any standard speed requirement. The fact remains, though, that the trotting ability is inherent to the breed, genetically transmitted to offspring. Nearly all harness racers found on the track today are standardbreds.

The registry's early standard that had to be met before racing required the standardbred to cover a mile (1.6 km) in two minutes and twenty seconds. Not only is enforcement of this standard obsolete, but the bloodline has also improved through the ages, enabling much faster speeds of well under two minutes.

Even though the standardbred inherits an inborn ability to trot or pace, its vast speed at these paces is the result of schooling. Without proper training, this horse, like any other, would be tempted to break the gait and speed into a gallop when insistently urged on. An artificial device—special shoes with weighted toe clips—causes the horse to lengthen its stride, while a different artificial innovation—a confining harness—discourages it from going into a gallop and breaking the pace of its stride.

The two gaits, trot and pace, are distinct. The trot is a two-beat gait with the diagonal legs moving together—left front and right hind, right front and left hind. Pacing, on the other hand, has the legs on the same side moving together—left fore with left hind, right fore with right hind. The trotter's strides are long and low, in contrast to the pacer's strides, which are more swaying. Pacers are generally faster than trotters. Although some lines of standardbreds do produce either trotters or pacers, the gait is decided in great part by special equipment, shoeing, and training.

The horse most responsible for the emergence of the breed was the Thoroughbred stallion Messenger, to which the standardbred directly traces its male line. Messenger had a pedigree that included all three of the Thoroughbred's Eastern ancestors, especially the Darley and Godolphin Arabians. In 1849, from a cross between Messenger and a Norfolk trotter mare that also had Messenger in its pedigree, came the stallion Hambleton. Hambleton and his offspring quickly dominated trotting races, overshadowing and effecting the extinction of almost all the other breeds. Nearly all trotters found on the track today trace their genesis back to Hambleton.

In appearance, the standardbred looks like a slightly smaller version of the Thoroughbred from which it is descended. Ranging from about fourteen to sixteen hands high, with a solid coat that's usually brown, black, bay, or chestnut, the standardbred is stockier than the Thoroughbred and has a less refined head. Its body is deep and long, with a high croup and powerful quarters.

Each year millions of American spectators attend standardbred harness races, which are under the auspices of the U.S. Trotting Association. This organization also serves as the breed's official registry.

THE AMERICAN STANDARDBRED IS KING OF THE HARNESS RACES IN AMERICA. HARNESS RACES ARE ENJOYED AT A NUMBER OF LEVELS AND LOCATIONS, INCLUDING THE ILLINOIS STATE FAIR, SHOWN HERE.

© Sally Klein

THE HORSE

M*organ*

The official horse of Vermont, the Morgan originated there as the result of the incredibly dominant gene pool of a single stallion, whose pedigree is a subject of speculation. This small stallion stood only about fourteen hands high, and was purchased in 1795 as a two-year-old by a Vermont singing teacher named Justin Morgan. The horse's name was Figure, but over time he came to be known simply as "Justin Morgan's horse"—and so developed the name of the breed.

Justin Morgan, like most of his contemporaries in a rural area, had to be somewhat of a jack-of-all-trades. It was not enough to teach singing lessons—Morgan also had to clear land and farm it for a livelihood. Consequently, he needed an all-around horse that could not only take him around the countryside to teach singing, but that could also assist him in clearing the land and plowing the fields. To fit this job description, the horse needed to have a temperament and gait that could produce a calm, smooth ride, and it also needed to have amply muscular conformation for stamina and strength to perform hard labor.

Justin Morgan's horse had every one of the desired traits. Despite its small height, it was a powerhouse capable of moving huge, heavy logs that much larger animals couldn't budge. Legend has it that Morgan entered the horse in countless log-pulling contests, and the horse never lost. Legend further holds that the animal was extremely quick, entered in many a race and winning every one.

But besides possessing enough versatility to be ideal for its owner, this stallion was also able to transmit those desirable traits to all of its progeny. The Morgan is unique, in fact, in being the only breed to descend from a single horse. No matter what kind of mare it was crossed with, the stallion imbued the offspring with its own outstanding qualities.

The breed enjoyed great popularity as a trotter until the 1850s. At that time, the standardbred became competition and soon dominated the track. The Morgan, in its pure form, was threatened with extinction, and, at this time, it was crossed with standardbreds for trotting speed and with Thoroughbreds for greater flash and a more comfortable ride.

In 1907, however, a farm was donated in Middlebury, Vermont, for the express purpose of propagating the Morgan as a breed, and its work continues even today. In addition, a few individual breeders in Vermont have taken an interest in returning the Morgan to its earlier bloodline and are breeding types that conform to Justin Morgan's horse. Morgans are entered in virtually every equestrian event, especially in Vermont, where they can still be found in all-Morgan harness races.

Today's Morgan is used primarily in two capacities—as a park horse and as a pleasure horse. Basically, the two types are not different in their conformation, only in their schooling, although some park horses do transmit their ability to their progeny. Park horses have a spirited, high-stepping trot and seem to enjoy their own animated "attitude," as it is called.

The Morgan is usually dark—a brown, black, or bay, or, less often, a chestnut. It stands from about 14.2 to 15.2 hands high and has a stocky, compact appearance with a thick barrel and big shoulders, and a short back and legs.

ABOVE: IN SADDLESEAT EQUITATION, THE MORGAN DISPLAYS A SPIRITED "ATTITUDE." OPPOSITE PAGE: THE MORGAN IS A STOCKY, COMPACT HORSE THAT STANDS FROM 14.2 TO 15.2 HANDS.

THE HORSE

Tennessee Walking Horse

Like the American saddlebred, the Tennessee walker was developed initially for transporting southern plantation owners and overseers on tours of the great estates. Often, these inspections were conducted in a field row by row, resulting in the horses sometimes being known as "turn row" horses.

Fairly tall, from fifteen to sixteen hands, the walker gives a splendidly smooth ride. Although it doesn't have the saddlebred's five gaits, it does possess two unique gaits—the flat walk and the renowned running walk. Both are loose four-beat gaits, with the head rising and falling in rhythmic nods with the regular fall of the hooves. The gaits' distinct movements derive from the horse's hind foot overstepping the print of the front foot. The running walk is performed at a much faster speed than the flat walk. At this swift, gliding gait, walkers can travel nine miles (14 km) in an hour. In addition to these two unique gaits, the walker takes poetic license with the canter, executing it in a distinct, rocking-chair style.

Artificial aids, the subject of controversy in recent times, have traditionally been employed to exaggerate the breed's natural overstep. On its own, the horse can overstride by about eighteen inches (45 cm); trained in special shoes, it can overstep by as much as fifty inches (125 cm). Painful mechanical devices or treatments to make the legs sore have been used in the past to enhance gaits, but these practices are now illegal according to the rules of the Tennessee Walking Horse Breeders Association and the American Horse Show Association. The horses' boots must be removed at shows, to check for evidence of illegal training practices.

Most often, the Tennessee walker is black, but it is possible for any color to be listed with the registry. The walker's head is plain and large, generally with wrinkled and sloping eyelids. Its powerful body, with well-muscled, sloping shoulders, a fairly long back, broad chest, and strong quarters, is not as refined as that of the saddlebred. Mane and tail are worn long and flowing.

The walker makes an ideal mount for beginning riders, thanks not only to its easy-to-ride gaits but also to its docile temperament. Although it appears extensively in the show ring, it is equally popular as a pleasure and trail horse, affording long hours of enjoyment ambling down country lanes.

It wasn't until 1935 that the breed's official registry was established, but earlier, by about 1910, the walker was informally recognized as its own breed. The walker is the result of selective breeding of Morgans, standardbreds, Thoroughbreds, and Arabs. Most walkers descend from a single stallion, Black Allan, which foaled in 1886 from a trotting stallion and a Morgan mare. Black Allan is recognized as the breed's foundation sire.

OPPOSITE PAGE: WITH TWO UNIQUE GAITS—A FLAT WALK AND THE CELEBRATED RUNNING WALK—THE TENNESSEE WALKING HORSE WAS INITIALLY DEVELOPED AS A COMFORTABLE MEANS OF TRANSPORTATION FOR OWNERS AND OVERSEERS OF PLANTATIONS IN THE SOUTHERN UNITED STATES.

THE HORSE

The Canadian Cutting Horse

Closely akin to the American quarter horse in both conformation and performance is the Canadian cutting horse. Standing a little taller than its American counterpart, at an average from 15.2 to 16.1 hands high, this breed was developed in Canada with the quarter horse as its primary foundation stock.

Like the quarter horse, the Canadian cutting horse is broad and muscular, with powerful hindquarters that enable it to turn on a dime with amazing quickness, then take off at a breakneck speed. This ability makes the horse well suited for working cattle—the reason for the breed's development in the first place.

Apparently, more is at work than conformation in predisposing the horse to work cattle. Again like the quarter horse, the Canadian cutting horse seems to have inherent "cow sense"—a trait that greatly simplifies life in the saddle for the Canadian rancher and professional cutting-horse competitor.

OPPOSITE PAGE: MOST TENNESSEE WALKERS ARE BLACK, BUT ANY COLOR IS ACCEPTABLE FOR LISTING WITH THE BREED'S REGISTRY. IT IS NOT UNUSUAL FOR WALKERS TO DISPLAY LARGE ROMAN NOSES. BELOW: NORTHERN COUSIN OF THE AMERICAN QUARTER HORSE, THE CANADIAN CUTTING HORSE SHARES THE SAME INBORN "COW SENSE" NECESSARY FOR CUTTING CATTLE, AS WELL AS THE SAME MUSCULAR, THOUGH TALLER, PHYSIQUE.

© Clix

THE GERMAN HANOVERIAN IS A GOLD MEDALIST IN OLYMPIC SHOW JUMPING, AS WELL AS IN INTERNATIONAL DRESSAGE EVENTS.

POPULAR EUROPEAN AND AUSTRALIAN BREEDS

Hanoverian

This legendary show horse is Germany's best-known breed, with an outstanding record in competitive show jumping and dressage. Ranging from 15.3 to 16.1 hands high, the solid-colored horse has taken gold medals in Olympic show jumping and in international dressage events.

The breed hails from an introduction of Thoroughbred blood into indigenous German studs beginning, according to earliest records, in 1714. With a strong, deep body, the Hanoverian is noted for its impulsion—great, ground-covering strides taken with elasticity and high energy that come from the shoulders and hocks with no high knee action. Hanoverians have been selectively bred for equestrian events since World War II.

© Norvia Behling

Holstein

Taller and heavier than the Hanoverian, with a neck that is slightly more arched, the Holstein is an old German breed that also has an outstanding record as a fierce competitor in equine sports. Recognized as important in the international horse community, the Holstein is exported all over the world. The United States recognized its stud book as long ago as 1892. The animal's ancestry goes all the way back to the Middle Ages, to those horses that carried off knights, charging into battle.

The breed's name derives from the region of Germany, the Schleswig-Holstein, where the bloodline first developed—the result of crossing Arab and Andalusian stallions with native mares. These horses were used primarily for military purposes. In the nineteenth century, the breed was infused with Cleveland bay and British Yorkshire coach blood to produce a quality carriage horse. Later, Thoroughbred blood was introduced to render a good riding horse.

Standing sixteen to seventeen hands high, found in all colors, Holsteiners are handsome, well-dispositioned all-purpose riding horses today. Only their height may rule them out as appropriate for some riders. Two of the most famous Holsteiners in history are Meteor, a great post-World War II show jumper, and Granat, a stellar dressage horse.

THE HOLSTEINER, AN OLD GERMAN BREED EXPORTED ALL OVER THE WORLD TO MEET THE DEMAND FOR IT IN THE SHOW RING, IS TALLER AND HEAVIER THAN THE HANOVERIAN.

© Sally Klein

Trakehner

Another German breed that has the respect of the international equestrian community is the Trakehner. Formerly know as the West Prussian, this animal, with its fine bones, chiseled head, and good action, is regarded as the most physically attractive of all the German breeds. Like the Holstein and Hanoverian, it performs well in show jumping, dressage, and eventing. It is also known for great heart. In the 1956 Stockholm Olympics, the Trakehner mare Halla carried her injured rider, who was unable to do anything but sit still in the saddle, through the entire show-jumping course to win the gold medal.

The breed was started in the early 1700s by Prussia's Frederick William I, who decided it was time to establish a stud in East Prussia. The breed's bloodline includes top-of-the-line Polish Arabians, which Frederick William imported, and native East Prussian breeds including the Schweiken. The Trakehner very nearly became extinct during World War II, when the Prussians tried to escape to the West with their prized horses as the Russians advanced. Only about 1,200 of the animals survived. Since then, the Germans have gone to great lengths to continue the breed, making it something of a national, rather than regional, horse.

WITH ITS CHISELED HEAD AND FINE BONE STRUCTURE, THE TRAKEHNER IS CONSIDERED THE MOST PHYSICALLY ATTRACTIVE OF THE GERMAN BREEDS.

© Norvia Behling

Swedish Warm-Blood

For the horse buyer who is not yet certain whether competitive showing or simple everyday riding will be demanded of the animal, the Swedish warm-blood is a virtually foolproof find. Its gentle temperament makes it safe for beginners, and its capability to master show skills renders it attractive even for the Olympic rider.

Standing about 16.2 hands high, the animal has a record as a top contender in international dressage. It has won Olympic medals, including the gold, in three-day eventing, and some Swedish warm-bloods possess special ability as hunters. The result of highly selective breeding beginning some three hundred years ago at Flyine, the breed, in more recent times, has been infused with Arab, Hanoverian, Thoroughbred, and Trakehner blood to maintain and improve its quality and performance.

AN IMPRESSIVE PRESENCE IN THE SHOW RING, THE SWEDISH WARM-BLOOD, STANDING ABOUT 16.2 HANDS HIGH, IS RENOWN FOR ITS ABILITY AT DRESSAGE.

Lipizzaner

This famous gray horse holds the world's attention for its dazzling, airborne movements, especially as taught by the Spanish Riding School of Vienna. The school and horse, in fact, are for all purposes synonymous. Originally descended from Spanish Andalusians, this breed was started by Austria's Archduke Charles II, who imported the Spanish horses to his country in order to found a stud at Lipizza (now Yugoslavia, but then a part of the Austrian empire). All records of the stud were destroyed during the Napoleonic Wars, and the breed's survival was a struggle.

Standing about 15.2 hands high, today's Lipizzaner is a master of haute école (high school riding). To awed crowds around the world, it performs with great grace and athleticism such stunning leaps as the croupade, courbette, and capriole.

ONE OF THE SHOWIEST AND MOST FAMOUS OF BREEDS, THE GRAY LIPIZZANER IS KNOWN FOR ITS MASTERY OF HAUTE ÉCOLE, ESPECIALLY FOR ITS AIRBORNE FEATS.

© Richard Day

Andalusian

The innate flamboyance of Spain's predominantly gray Andalusian makes it a natural, like the Lipizzaner, that its bloodline helped to produce, at haute école. Resulting from a cross of native Spanish mares and Barb stallions, the Andalusian had the prestige for years of being Europe's most popular riding horse. Today, however, the horse buyer in North America or Europe would find it extremely difficult to locate an Andalusian for sale.

PROGENITOR OF THE LIPIZZANER, THE SPANISH ANDALUSIAN ONCE HAD THE DISTINCTION OF BEING EUROPE'S MOST POPULAR RIDING HORSE, A POSITION LONG SINCE USURPED BY OTHER BREEDS.

© Sally Klein

The Waler

Because there are no indigenous horses in Australia, European settlers there in the late eighteenth century were left with no option other than importation. The first imported horses were from South Africa, then Europe. The continent's own saddle horse, the Waler, was developed from crosses of these imported breeds. Hack mares were bred with Thoroughbred, Arabian, and Anglo-Arabian stallions to produce the new breed—which, at its best, looks much like the Thoroughbred.

The Waler derives its name from New South Wales—the name broadly assigned to all newly settled parts of Australia in the early days of colonization. Even though the expanse was eventually divided into smaller states, each with its own name, the term "Waler" seems fit for this breed, which really is a national— or continental—treasure.

Standing an average of sixteen hands high, the Waler has the good stamina and decent temperament to make an all-purpose saddle horse. Its role in the development of Australia cannot be overstated. With its incredible stamina and hardiness, the Waler was indispensable to colonists forging through the arid deserts, craggy mountains, and formidable grasslands. In sheer endurance, the breed is on record as having outdistanced and outlasted the camel in desert campaigns of World War I, during which time the Waler was exported to India and Europe.

With the decline of the cavalry at the end of World War I, the Waler also declined as a breed, and today it is very nearly extinct.

© Richard Day

© FPG International

TOP: IT IS NOT SURPRISING THAT HUMANS HAVE
BEEN CAPTIVATED FOR MILLENNIA BY THE
HORSE, GIVEN ITS SPIRIT AND THE SHEER POWER
OF ITS PRESENCE. BOTTOM: IN AUSTRALIA, AS
ON THE RANCH LANDS OF THE UNITED STATES
AND CANADA, RANCHERS MOVE HORSES AS PART
OF THE JOB.

WILD AS A BRUMBY

If, in a fit of temper someday, you overhear someone bark the term "brumby" in your direction, take comfort in knowing you have not been cursed. Rather, someone has metaphorically likened your behavior to that of the Brumby, Australia's wild horse.

No one knows for sure, but common sense would indicate that the term for this intractable horse originated from the aboriginal word, "baroomby," which means wild.

The Brumby is small, standing no taller than fifteen hands high. Its wildness is not to be equated with its being indigenous to Australia; it is not, for Australia has no native horses. Like the American wild Mustang, the Brumby started off as a domesticated animal. Various breeds of domesticated horses were imported to Australia from Europe and South Africa and were then turned free to roam and breed at will on the continent's wide-open ranch land in the mid-1800s, during the gold rush. The wild Brumby thus developed. Its numbers increased so dramatically that, for a time, efforts were made to destroy it. Though Brumby horses are still to be found in the more remote desert or mountain regions, mainly in the Northern Territory, they are not protected. If found grazing on someone's grasslands, they are commonly shot.

After more than a century of inbreeding, the horse has continued to decline in conformation and temperament. It has also developed an antipathy towards humans that cannot be overcome by efforts at domestication.

When called a Brumby, then, you may be suffering an insult on more grounds than just your fiery temper. Your looks and emotional adjustment to society may also be in question.

CHAPTER FIVE

Equestrian Sports

© Alice Garik

*But he, mighty man, lay mightily in the
whirl of dust, forgetful of his horsemanship!*
Homer, The Iliad

SLEIGH RIDING IS A MODERN VERSION OF ONE OF THE EARLIEST INTERACTIONS BETWEEN HUMANS AND THE DOMESTICATED HORSE: THE FIRST HORSE WAS DOMESTICATED TO PULL A CONVEYANCE, NOT TO BE RIDDEN.

Early in history, humans appreciated the horse as a means of transportation, an essential element in battle, and a helpmate in heavy labor. Given the horse's established presence in all the vital activities of early humans, and given its innate beauty and majesty and the attendant thrill those qualities lend the human half of the human-horse duo, it can be seen as inevitable that we would eventually look again to the horse when devising amusement for our precious leisure time.

The horse in sports dates to prehistoric times, when two drivers (horses were driven before they were ridden) first realized they could challenge one another through the speed of a horse. After chariot racing but still before the time of Christ came another ancient equestrian sport, a ball-and-mallet game that was the precursor of today's polo. The Olympic sport of dressage, which really just entails advanced schooling of the horse, has evolved since Xenophon's documentation of it about 380 B.C. (the earliest extant record) into the highly sophisticated athletic art form that we know today.

Although equestrian sports, like all others, are constantly undergoing a subtle form of revisement and refinement, it is a serious mistake to assume that our generation is in any way original or ingenious in incorporating the horse in sport. With today's mass media providing unprecedented exposure to equine events, horse sports undoubtedly are growing in popularity at a rate that keeps apace with the public's consciousness. But in its essence, the tradition of equestrian sport is as old as the first partnership between humans and horses.

HARNESS RACING

When the drivers of two-wheeled, lightweight sulkies round the bend of their oval racecourses, they are reenacting a prehistoric event—by far the most ancient of all equestrian sports. Early humans first domesticated the horse to be driven, not ridden (ancient horses were too small to accommodate humans on their backs); their competitive instincts, as well as their evolving desire for pageantry and showmanship, meant that chariot racing was not long in the making.

Although the sport of harness racing is essentially atavistic, recalling its prototype from more than a millenium ago, today's expression of the event has its own distinct articulation. The chariot races of long ago were performed at a gallop, the horse's fastest gait. Today's races, however, are executed at a slightly slower speed—the gaits of the trot or the pace.

Both the trot and the pace are two-beat gaits, whereas the gallop is four-beat, with each hoof striking the ground individually. The trot involves each pair of diagonal legs—the off-fore and near-hind, near-fore and off-hind—striking the ground together to propel the horse forward in two beats.

Although it is also a two-beat gait, the pace differs from the trot in that it has the same-side hooves striking at the same time—near-fore and near-hind legs moving together, and off-fore and off-hind legs moving together. The pace is also a slightly faster gait.

THE HORSE

Over time, these two-beat gaits proved favorites for harness racing because they afford to the driver more control over the animal (it's difficult to feel in control with nothing but reins connecting you to a horse galloping at breakneck speed), and they spare the animal the unnecessary strain and quick tiring of the faster, more strenuous gallop. Harness races as we know them today are a fairly recent development, originating in the early 1800s as sport among southern U.S. plantation owners, who used trotters and pacers as an efficient and comfortable means of surveying their vast landholdings.

Trotting breeds themselves were in existence long before the landed gentry of nineteenth-century America had the notion to engage them in sport. European trotters predate the Thoroughbred and are thought to have been brought to Britain in 1015 from Denmark. It was America's development of the standardbred, the harness racer par excellence, in the mid-1800s that precipitated the rapid growth of the sport—and that cleared the field of most other breeds of trotters. Other breeds simply could not compete.

The standardbred's entire purpose, from earliest breeding, was to be a trotting and pacing horse, not a riding horse. The name of the breed points to this function: in 1879, a "standard" distance of travel within a set time was a prerequisite for a horse to enter trotting races. Although such a standard is no longer required, the breed itself continues to dominate the harness racecourse.

TODAY'S HARNESS RACING INVOKES THE CHARIOT RACES OF OLD—BY FAR THE MOST ANCIENT OF ALL EQUESTRIAN SPORTS. CONTEMPORARY HARNESS RACES ARE CONDUCTED AT A TROT OR PACE, WHEREAS THE ANCIENT CHARIOT RACES WERE HELD AT A GALLOP.

© MacDonald/Envision

Dressage

The French word *dressage* derives from the verb *dresser*, which means to teach or to school, specifically an animal. In its connotations, however, the word goes far beyond a reference to simplistic kinds of training. It presupposes a certain level of advancement that involves a sophisticated communication between the human and the animal being schooled. Henry Wynmalen, in *Dressage—A Study of the Finer Points of Riding*, explains dressage by describing what it would mean if applied to other kinds of animal schooling: "Thus the ordinary house-training of a dog, teaching him to come when called and to comply with similar fundamental rules of doggy behavior does not qualify as dressage, but the training of a gundog, or a sheep or police dog or that of a performing dog in the circus certainly does, for that is dressage."

The advanced schooling of the horse that is dressage develops the animal's natural abilities—its movements—and refines them so that they become perfectly balanced. To think of the dressage horse, it may be helpful to look at a parallel among our own species. Anyone can walk a straight line. But the gymnast who walks a straight line on a balance beam, effortlessly executing double-back flips and handstands with great grace and control, takes a basic human ability and transforms it into something magical. The same is true of horses. Any horse can go through the four basic gaits—walk, trot, canter, gallop. But the dressage horse executes these gaits with the amazing grace and presence that emanate from perfect balance and precision. And like its gymnast counterpart, the dressage horse goes far beyond these basics to perform feats few can accomplish—lateral movements such as the passage, or even those breathtaking "airs above the ground" such as the capriole and croupade, leaping movements for which the Spanish Riding School of Vienna's Lipizzaners are famous. The Fédération Equestre Internationale's rule book describes the purpose of dressage as "the harmonious development of the physique and ability of the horse" so that it becomes "calm, supple, loose, and flexible" and "confident, attentive, and keen."

Anyone who spends any time at all working with horses engages in a kind of basic dressage, usually in preparation for some other equestrian activity. For those who pursue dressage as an end in itself, the discipline is something quite different. In competitive dressage, a memorized "test" is ridden before judges in an arena that is marked at intervals along the outside ring by twelve letters and is mentally marked by five imaginary letters down the center. The test involves moving from point to point at specific gaits and executing movements precisely at the letter markings.

One of the beauties of dressage is its quality of open-endedness. The neophyte horseperson can begin dressage, enjoy it, and grow in horsemanship. At the other end of the spectrum, the seasoned rider, no matter how well he or she performs in dressage competition, can always find some area of weakness in the horse's schooling that merits further attention.

In the Olympic and World Championship dressage events, two demanding tests are used—the FEI Grand Prix, lasting seven minutes, and the Grand Prix

In the choice of a horse and a wife, a man must please himself, ignoring the opinion and advice of friends.

George John Whyte-Melville,
Riding Recollections

Opposite page: This horse performs the piaffe—a collected, in-place trot involving no forward motion—as part of its dressage competition.

EQUESTRIAN SPORTS

Special, a seven-and-a-half-minute test with all the transitions and movements of the Grand Prix but in a scrambled order. The twelve top riders from the Grand Prix compete in the Special, whose scores alone are used for awarding individual medals.

The Grand Prix test requires a rider to go through all of the school paces, including a collected, extended, and free walk; and collected, medium, and extended trot and canter. Classic movements such as the passage, an exaggerated high-stepping, rhythmic trot, and the piaffe, a collected, in-place trot (with no forward motion), as well as half-passes, pirouettes, and flying changes of lead are also required. In all, the test has thirty-six numbered movements and a total possible score of 430, with each movement judged from 0 to 10 and some counting double. In addition to the scoring of individual movements, a collective score is given based on the horse's overall impulsion, submission, and paces, and on the rider's seat and position.

Dressage, in its advanced levels, is by far the most complex, cerebral, and aesthetically pleasing of all equestrian sports. But it is essentially a subtle activity, and thus, is not necessarily a runaway crowd pleaser for the masses. It does not possess the pyrotechnics of show jumping, the thrill of the race, or the rough-and-tumble excitement of polo, and, therefore, does not yet enjoy as much widespread popularity as these other equestrian events. But with the advent of the freestyle dressage competition, which is ridden to music, the sport promises to become more accessible in its appeal.

DRESSAGE IS THE MOST ELEGANT, SUBTLE, AND COMPLEX OF ALL THE EQUESTRIAN SPORTS.

POLO

In terms of sheer prestige (and certainly ruggedness), polo is without peer among horse sports. Since its beginning, it has been associated with royalty, becoming egalitarian only insofar as it eventually spread to include those who were merely rich. Even today, with television's democratization of once-rarefied sports worlds, and with the burgeoning sophistication of the masses, polo as a participant sport remains well outside the realm of the average person. The expense of owning and continually replacing and upgrading the several ponies necessary for playing the game is prohibitive enough for most people.

Polo, one of the oldest horse sports and the world's first sport ever to be played with a ball and a stick, began as a source of amusement for the royal courts of Asia and Asia Minor as long ago as 600 B.C. Chinese and Persian paintings and writings document its existence as a contest between two teams for possession of a ball, which was then hit with a long-handled mallet to one end of a large, open field, and then through the opposing team's goalpost. The word *polo* is a derivative of the Tibetan *pu-lu*, which means willow root—the substance from which the ball is made.

Unlike contemporary polo, the earliest form of the game was much more of a spectacle than a pure sport. Hundreds of ponies were employed and players were attired in resplendent costumes. Interestingly, the ancient event was not dominated by males, as is today's adaptation; women had their own teams.

POLO DATES BACK TO AS LONG AGO AS 600 B.C., WHEN THE ROYAL COURTS OF ASIA AND ASIA MINOR ENGAGED IN A BALL-AND-STICK GAME ON HORSEBACK.

With the fall of the Moghul empire, the game dwindled in popularity. The only region in which it remained vital was India's Himalayan hinterlands, and it was there that British officers and colonists discovered it and made it their own in the 1850s. The wealthy British plantation owners and high-ranking cavalrymen played the sport, along with Indian nobility, as a favorite leisure activity. Shortly after polo received this elixir from the British, Indian officers, happy to see their native game so warmly received and resuscitated, took steps of their own to ensure its longevity. In 1859, they founded the Silchar Club in Kashmir—the world's first polo club. Just ten years later, the first match was played in Britain, and in 1875, the Hurlington Club was created in Britain to standardize the game with rules and regulations.

While polo was being enthusiastically embraced in England, it was also spreading to other parts of the world, thanks to its new British practitioners. English and Irish settlers in Argentina brought the game there, where it remains strong today, producing some of the world's best advanced (high-goal) players and ponies. Britons established the game throughout their empire, in South Africa, Australia, New Zealand, and other locations where there were British military bases, making it for many years a game of the military's upper echelons.

Polo's introduction to North America was purely civilian, though still very much the domain of the elite. In 1876, just one year after Britain established the Hurlington Club, James Gordon Bennett returned from a stint in England, loaded down with enough mallets and balls for all of his New York friends to learn to play the game. Bennett was hardly a member of the working class; as a newspaper publisher, yachtsman, and financier of Stanley's quest for Livingston in Africa and of an Arctic expedition, he ensured that the sport was shared with persons like himself—the freewheeling rich. These artistocratic Americans soon formed the country's first polo club—the Westchester Polo Club in Newport, Rhode Island—and the game spread in popularity all along the Eastern Seaboard. By 1855, students at Harvard were playing polo.

After its rapid spread from country to country, almost like a contagion, polo suffered its share of hard times. World War II took a toll on the game in Britain, but due to the efforts of Lord Cowdray in the 1950s, it survived. Lord Cowdray's friend, Lord Mountbatten, was another enthusiast of the game. As the uncle and mentor of Prince Philip, he ensured royal interest in the sport, which Philip passed on, scepter-style, to his son Prince Charles.

In the United States, the game was revived by a number of the leisure class, who propagated it in all reaches of the country, from California to Texas. In Texas, at least for a while, the sport was played according to a different sort of decorum: in cowboy clothes, from atop a western saddle. By the 1970s, however, even in Texas, polo had conformed to a more homogeneous international game, there being little difference between the appearance of the players at Dallas' Willow Bend club or those in Florida's Boca Raton.

In 1983, the game was finally formalized as an international sport by the creation of the International Polo Federation. It was no coincidence that the organization was headquartered in Buenos Aires. There, in the midst of vast cattle ranches and fortunes, both of which meant a ready pool of polo ponies and players,

ABOVE: POLO SPREAD THROUGHOUT THE BRITISH EMPIRE AND ENGLISH-SPEAKING WORLD SOON AFTER ITS ADOPTION BY THE BRITISH MILITARY OFFICERS IN INDIA IN THE 1850S. POLO IS A FAVORITE OF BRITAIN'S PRINCE CHARLES. OPPOSITE PAGE: EXTREMELY STRENUOUS FOR THE PONIES THAT PARTICIPATE, POLO DEMANDS EVEN GREATER SKILLS FROM THE HORSES THAN IT DOES FROM RIDERS. MANY TOP PLAYERS, IN FACT, SAY THE GAME HINGES ON THE HORSES.

© Popperfoto/Langrish

© Richard Day

POLO PLAYERS WEARING THE NUMBER FOUR PLAY DEFENSIVE BACK (THE OTHER DEFENSIVE POSITION IS NUMBER THREE). PLAYER FOUR IS THE TEAM'S POWERHOUSE, RESPONSIBLE FOR DRIVING THE BALL DOWNFIELD.

the game had become a favorite national sport, challenged only by soccer. Young children and seasoned professionals alike play polo in Argentina, both casually and with great hoopla—much as baseball and football are played in the United States. As early as 1924, in fact, Argentina had reached supremacy in its polo-playing stature—a position it has held ever since. That year, the first in which polo was a part of the Olympic games, the Argentine team won. Many of today's best ten-goal players—the highest ranking in the game—hail from the South American country.

© Alice Garik

The game itself is fast and furious, usually played from the back of a small Thoroughbred or Thoroughbred cross, generally one that is under 15.2 hands high. Until 1912, the mount was actually required to be pony height—that is, under 14.2 hands high. Any breed will do for playing polo, but the more serious the game, the more likely it is to be played off a Thoroughbred. The experience and ranking of the player largely determine the age of the horse. For average club play, the horse will usually be close to twelve years old and seldom younger than seven. A seasoned professional player will ride a younger horse for greater speed. In advanced polo, the average age of the horse is about five or six; ridden for only one period of a match, a horse as young as three or four years old may even be used. The disparity between the ages of the mounts used in club play and those on the professional, international circuit is only one sign of the differences between the two levels of the game. The game's execution is distinctly different, too—club polo being something akin to hockey on horseback, international polo being a finely calibrated sport of both mental and physical finesse.

Played on a field that is three hundred yards (274 m) long by two hundred yards (183 m) wide, the game is divided into "chukkers"—periods that are seven and a half minutes long, separated by three-minute outs and a five-minute halftime. Average club polo consists of four or less chukkers, while high-goal matches last six chukkers. Top-ranking Argentina plays eight-chukker matches.

The game begins with two teams of four players each facing one another in the middle of the field. A referee rolls the ball, either made of willow root or plastic, between the teams to begin the action. The teams strive to drive the ball down the field with long mallets always carried in their right hands and into the opposing team's goalposts. After each score, teams reassemble in line in the middle of the field to begin again, this time changing goalposts. Should the score be tied at the end of the last chukker, a sudden-death chukker is played, with the first team to score the winner.

Because of its quick-scramble speed all over the field, the game isn't as amenable to television coverage as are most other horse sports. Nor is it simple enough for the novice spectator to follow easily. The four players on each team have definite positions, but the nature of the sport demands that players have the alacrity and flexibility to change roles with a teammate in a split second, as the plays necessitate.

Offensive players are numbers 1 and 2. Number 2 sets up the play for number 1, who is responsible for driving the ball through the goalpost. Numbers 3 and 4 are defensive players. Number 3, often the captain and most skilled member of the team, serves as strategist, planning the plays and feeding the ball to the offensive players. Player number 4 is the defensive back and is characteristically the largest member of the team, who rides the largest horse and has the most power to move the ball downfield.

Riding at fast speeds, not uncommonly of up to forty miles (64 km) per hour, players swing their forty-nine- to fifty-three-inch (123- to 133-cm) bamboo mallets in one of eight shots: forward, backward, and diagonal shots swung from either the left (near) or right (off) side of the horse; an under-the-pony's-neck swing taken at a ninety-degree angle to the horse's body; and a similar swing taken

TO STAY ON THE BALL, THE POLO PONY MUST HAVE GREAT AGILITY—THE ABILITY TO TURN ON A DIME WHENEVER NECESSARY.

under the tail. For the defensive player, hooking the opponent's mallet with his or her own on the same side as the ball is an important play, but cross-hooking over or under the opponent's horse is a serious offense.

Given the vast speeds, abrupt turns and stops, and the ponies' side-by-side races to the ball with inevitable collisions, it is little wonder that the sport frequently proves injurious to both human and horse. The stress placed on the ponies necessitates that they are used for only a limited period of the game; each player must have several different ponies to ride in order to participate in a single match. (This requirement to own not one, but many ponies automatically serves as a screening device, filtering out those would-be players who lack the expendable income to purchase the "equipment.") For the players, polo is equally unsparing. Breaks and concussions are simply one of the game's realities.

The role the pony plays in the success of the player and team is inordinate. Professionals attribute 75 percent of their game to the ability of their animals.

© Alice Garik

But the true test of skill with the horse comes long before players assemble for a game; it occurs in the training of the ponies. Here is the opportunity to take a horse with good potential and make it great. Especially important in the training is the creation of a soft mouth—one that will respond immediately to the rider's slightest cue to the reins. With the groundwork for their mounts thus laid in training, players don't really have to have dazzling riding skills. Although they certainly must be adept, athletic riders with a balanced seat, they need not possess the knowledge or skills of a dressage rider, who can effect sophisticated movements and responses from a horse with subtle use of aids—that is, through the rider's seat, legs, and hands. Outfitted with a good pony, a player has the freedom to concentrate on mallet shots and play strategies. The best players, as well as being aggressive sportspersons, however, tend to be accomplished equestrians. The most experienced ten-goal players prefer training their own ponies in many cases, rather than entrusting that critical task to anyone else.

Emily, I've a little confession to make. I really am a horse doctor. But marry me, and I'll never look at any other horse!
Groucho Marx, A Day at the Races

© Alice Garik

© Jack Casement/Envision

ABOVE: HARDLY THE BEER AND PRETZEL SET, THIS RACING CROWD INCLUDES ENGLAND'S ROYAL FAMILY, WHICH ALWAYS TURNS OUT FOR THE ROYAL ASCOT HELD EACH JUNE NEAR WINDSOR CASTLE. BELOW: THE SEAT OF THE JOCKEY WAS IN CONTACT WITH THE SADDLE IN RACING'S EARLY DAYS, UNTIL THE FORWARD (RAISED AND CROUCHED) SEAT WAS RIDDEN IN THE 1879 DERBY BY WINNING JOCKEY TED SLOAN. *THREE STUDIES OF A MOUNTED JOCKEY* (C. 1866-1868) BY EDGAR DEGAS PREDATES THE FORWARD SEAT, WHICH IS STILL USED TODAY ON THE TRACK. OPPOSITE PAGE: ONE OF THE MOST EXCITING MOMENTS IN EQUESTRIAN SPORTS IS THE START OF THE THOROUGHBRED RACE.

RACING

Horse racing may well be the most egalitarian of equine sports, attracting every echelon of society from royalty and aristocracy to blue-collar working class. The idea of competing for speed on horse is ancient. But racing in the form we know it today, involving a regulation flat track, did not evolve until the seventeenth century in England, during the Restoration (1660–1688). Earlier in England, during the reign of Henry VIII, horses were raced at Chester. The first permanent racetrack was created in 1605 at Newmarket by James I, and Charles I frequented it often—even issuing the decree that precipitated the English Civil War from Newmarket in 1642. But it was after that, under Charles II, that racing really developed into a national passion. Known as the Father of the British Turf, Charles II was not only a great fan of racing and the pleasure it afforded him as a spectator, he was also a participant in the sport—the only member of the royal family to hold that distinction until 1985, when Princess Anne debuted as an amateur jockey. Charles II founded the Newmarket Town Plate, which remains to this day England's oldest race still being run. (Newmarket was also the place where the first Jockey Club was founded in 1752 by a group of aristocrats who drafted racing rules and calendars and maintained the stud book. It remains England's ruling body for racing with, in fact, the same family—the Weatherbys—overseeing the administrative matters.)

Royal patronage for racing continued after Charles II. In 1711, Queen Anne had a racetrack built near Windsor Castle on Ascot Heath, where the Royal Ascot continues to be held each June, attended by the royal family. Even today, Queen Elizabeth is an avid and informed racing enthusiast, with her own horses on the track and, often, in the winner's circle.

Beginning at the close of the nineteenth century, British racing caught the world's attention. Americans traveled to England to race, as well as to buy and train the British Thoroughbreds that have dominated racing since the breed's establishment in the late 1600s. It was an American jockey racing in England in the 1879 Derby who changed forever the form of the race. Ted Sloan, the first jockey ever to ride up from the saddle in a crouched position known as the forward seat, won the Derby amid the jeers of the established British racing community. Soon, though, British jockeys and all others around the world were following suit, riding with this more efficient seat.

At precisely the same time racing was developing in England, the British colonists in the New World were ensuring its spread there. The first racetrack in America was created in 1665 on Long Island by the British governor of New York. The American wilderness demanded real dedication on the part of racing enthusiasts, for clearing the land for a racing area was no small accomplishment. Because of the formidable task this clearing entailed, most of the straightaways were relatively short—only up to a quarter mile (400 m). This racing condition required specific skills from the horses, with sprinting more important than long-distance speed. The American quarter horse developed as a breed in the eastern states to answer this need.

EQUESTRIAN SPORTS

It were not best that we should all think alike; it is difference of opinion that makes horse races.

  Mark Twain, Pudd'nhead Wilson

But the quarter-mile races and the quarter horse that ran them did not preclude the longer races run by Thoroughbreds in America, especially as civilization tamed the wilderness. In 1867, the Belmont Stakes—first of the prestigious Triple Crown races to be founded—debuted in New York. A long race, now shortened to one and a half miles (2.4 km) from its original two miles (3.2 km), it is the last of the famous three to be run during a year's racing schedule. Not long after the Belmont Stakes, the other two Triple Crown races were inaugurated, this time in the South. In 1873, the first Preakness was run in Maryland, followed two years later by the Kentucky Derby. Run by three-year-old Thoroughbreds, the Triple Crown is the zenith of racing in America, providing thrill not only for die-hard fans but also for the masses, primarily as a result of much media coverage and hype. The infrequent occurrence of a single horse taking all three events in a year creates a major sensation across the country. Triple Crown winners such as Gallant Fox (1930), Secretariat (winner in 1973, a full twenty-five years since another horse had won all three), and Seattle Slew (the 1977 winner, and the first horse undefeated in any race) are equine athletes with a place carved in history.

  These days, Thoroughbred racing has become a truly international sport, following an identical set of rules and regulations wherever it is held, be it North America, Britain, or France. One standard observed worldwide pertains to the horses' age. The minimum legal age for racing a Thoroughbred is two years. As the horse enters its third year, its challenges on the track increase. The most prestigious races such as America's Triple Crown are limited to three-year-old horses.

EQUESTRIAN SPORTS

Northwind Picture Archives

THE STEEPLECHASE, WHICH WAS OFFICIALLY RECORDED FOR THE FIRST TIME IN 1752 IN IRELAND, EVOLVED FROM THE BRITISH EMPIRE'S POPULAR FOX HUNT. AFTER BRITAIN ENACTED THE ENCLOSURE ACTS, WHICH CAUSED FENCES TO BE ERECTED AROUND PREVIOUSLY OPEN GROUNDS, HUNTERS HAD TO JUMP FENCES IN ORDER TO KEEP UP WITH THEIR PACK OF HOUNDS. THIS SPORT LED TO THE JUMPING RACES KNOWN AS STEEPLECHASES.

STEEPLECHASE

Steeplechasing, racing horses a set distance over a course studded with fences and a body of water that requires jumping, was first recorded as an event in Ireland in 1752. The name derived from the landmarks chosen to delineate the race's starting and finishing points: church steeples—the most easily visible landmarks in the Irish countryside.

The sport began as a natural evolution from fox hunting. In the British Isles, until the mid-1700s, agricultural land was unfenced, with open-range grazing. Fox hunters on their horses could pursue their hounds with little impediment, save a few ditches or streams to jump. But in the mid-1700s things changed. Britain enacted its Enclosure Acts, suddenly changing the face of the countryside. Fox hunters, to stay after their game, now had to leap fences on horseback. Racing under these conditions soon followed as an amusing, challenging pastime.

The sport spread swiftly outside the British Isles, wherever Britain had colonies and especially wherever flat racing was already a well-established sport. The nineteenth century was a time of fast growth for the steeplechase. And by the turn of the twentieth century, steeplechasing had attained a distinct personality among equine sports—one that has been retained even to the present. Although the steeplechase doesn't require the vast wealth necessary to participate on a serious level as does Thoroughbred flat racing, in a sense, it is a more elitist sport. Steeplechasing tends to be the pastime of old money—a relatively closed set not often penetrated by newcomers. Also, whereas flat racing can be the game of anyone with enough money, regardless of whether they know the off from the near side of a horse, steeplechasing is for pure horsepersons—an elitism of its own that has nothing to do with money per se. And while there's money to be made at the sport, it is nowhere near the gargantuan amounts that are available in classic flat racing. Steeplechasing is somewhat akin to a pedigree—it is a given, like an educated parent's expectation for his or her children to attend college, that is handed on among families from generation to generation.

FOX HUNTING, THOUGH NOT AS COMMON AS IT ONCE WAS, REMAINS AN AMUSING PASTIME FOR THE ELITE, AS WELL AS FOR A FACTION OF EQUESTRIANS WHO SIMPLY ENJOY THE SPORT.

Simon Bruty/Allsport

THE HORSE

Common usage of the word *steeplechase* today has rendered it, in most instances, a misnomer. Most people associate a steeplechase with any kind of jumping race. In fact, jumping races can be broken down into three categories, only one of which, the "brush" race, is a steeplechase. Brush races require a two-to-four-mile (3.2-to-6.4-km) course that includes one water jump, one ditch fence per mile, and a minimum of twelve fences in the first two miles (3.2 km) of the race. The other two jumping races often generically called steeplechase are hurdle races and timber races. Hurdle races put the emphasis on speed, rather than on clean jumps, and are often an alternate career for Thoroughbreds that can't make it on the flat track. Hurdle races also represent an initiation for three-year-olds into jumping. The hurdles are thin rails that slant in the direction of the finish. Timber races, on the other hand, are more akin to fox hunting, and, in fact, have hunting experience as a prerequisite. The obstacles in timber races—also known as point-to-points—are post-and-rail fences, perhaps with a fence-capped stone wall intermixed.

Most steeplechase horses get their start in speed jumping through hurdle races. They run hurdles as three- or four-year-olds, then advance to steeplechase the following year. In Ireland, where the event got its start, the steeplechase remains a major national sport, warmly embraced by a knowledgeable and spirited public.

OPPOSITE PAGE: IN THE STEEPLECHASE, HORSES ARE RACED OVER A COURSE THAT CONTAINS FENCES AND A BODY OF WATER THAT REQUIRES JUMPING. BELOW LEFT: STEEPLECHASE JOCKEYS WEIGH IN BEFORE THE RACE, JUST AS FLAT RACE JOCKEYS DO. BELOW: BEGINNING WITH ITS CALL TO POST, THE STEEPLECHASE HAS AN ATTENDANT ELITISM THAT HAS NOTHING TO DO WITH MONEY PER SE.

© MacDonald/Envision

SHOW JUMPING ALSO OWES ITS ORIGIN TO THE
FOX HUNT, DEVELOPING AS A SPORT IN ITS OWN
RIGHT IN THE SECOND HALF OF THE 1700S. BY
THE FIRST HALF OF THE NINETEENTH CENTURY,
IT HAD BECOME EXTREMELY POPULAR.

SHOW JUMPING

Like the steeplechase, show jumping grew out of the hunt. Once the British Isles'
Enclosure Acts meant fences had to be jumped when keeping up with the pack
of hounds, it wasn't long before the hunters began jumping "in cold blood"—the
Georgian-era term popular for describing any jump not necessitated by the hunt
itself. What started as fun in the mid- to late 1700s became the epitome of fashion
in the first half of the nineteenth century.

Originally known as "leaping contests" instead of show jumping, the
events were officially recorded in the second half of the nineteenth century,
with Paris documenting the first in 1866, followed by Dublin in 1868, Isling-
ton's (London) Royal in the 1870s, and New York's National in 1883. The
first truly international show-jumping competition occurred in 1902 at the
Turin Horse Show. Riding his high jumper Meloppa, the champion of the
show was Italy's Captain Federico Caprilli, who was responsible for the forward
seat (raised in a crouch, up from the saddle) becoming standard form in jumping
contests. The Stockholm Olympics of 1912 marked the first time show jumping
became an important event. That year, a French military officer took the gold,
establishing a precedent for show jumping as the dominion of the military—
a trend that continued for forty years.

Concurrent with the loosening of the military's stranglehold on show jumping in the 1950s came the advent of television, a phenomenon that was primarily
responsible for show jumping's skyrocketing popularity. Show jumping, as a fairly
obvious sport in which such subtleties as a well-turned hock or correct lead aren't
an issue, is especially amenable to camera coverage: either the jump is cleared or
it's not, and the guesswork is minimal, for an uncleared fence wall will fall and
an uncleared stream will certainly create a splash.

The rules of show jumping, too, are conducive to an easy understanding
of the sport by the masses. International standards have a penalty of four faults
issued for any fence that is knocked down or any stream not cleared. Refusal at
a jump scores three faults for the first offense, six for the second, and elimina-
tion from the competition should there be a third refusal to jump. Speed, too,
is a factor, along with precision of execution. (Of course this is not a race, like
steeplechasing, in which all contenders run at the same time, but of individual
performances of one horse at a time.) Should horses have equal scores on jumps,
the winner is the animal/rider team to have finished the course in the shortest
time. In addition, each jump bears an allocated amount of time in which it can
be cleared without a fault being incurred. Each second that elapses in excess of
the allotted time results in a one-quarter fault.

The largest purse among show-jumping events is the Grand Prix. To
win, a horse must clear the course with no faults, then return for a second round
cleared, again, with no faults, on a shorter course with higher and wider fences.
Winning a major Grand Prix is a significant accomplishment for both horse
and rider, and watching one is among the most exciting of equestrian sports
for spectators.

The Nations' Cup and World Championship represent the pinnacle of challenge and achievement for show jumpers. The 1986 World Championship stands among the most dramatic of all sports upsets. A female rider, Gail Greenough of Canada, astounded both the competition and the crowd by winning with a perfect score against tough competition, which included a United States Olympic silver medalist and other top contenders from across the world. Her horse, Mister T, a medium-sized Hanoverian/Thoroughbred cross, carried her to a win that left the closest competition behind with eight faults, and the next with ten faults. Not only was Greenough's performance a thrilling moment in jumping history, it was one that decidedly declared the place of women in the sport.

With a steady percentage increase of better horses and better riders, the sport of show jumping continues to gain in popularity and prestige. As the darling of the television camera, it promises to hold its own before the masses.

THIS TOKYO EVENT UNDERSCORES THE FACT THAT SHOW JUMPING TRULY IS AN INTERNATIONAL SPORT, CONTINUING TO RISE IN POPULARITY AND PRESTIGE, WITH INCREASING TELEVISION COVERAGE.

*R*odeo, *the only equestrian sport performed with western instead of English saddle and tack, traces its origins to the workplace: to the hardscrabble cattle ranches, where more of a working cowboy's life was spent in the saddle than out, and where the job demanded special skills not only of the cowboy, but of the horse as well. Unlike the trotters of the southern plantations, for whom a day's work only meant providing a comfortable and quick ride for the landowners and their overseers, the ranching horse's day was rough-and-tumble. It required good footing and sensibilities through arduous terrain, sprinting and quick-turning abilities, and an almost inborn skill at working cattle that was manifested as an intuitive knowledge of when and how to head off, round up, and keep cantankerous cattle in line.*

At the same time that cowboys were active in America's West, stockmen of the nineteenth century were facing similar, if not greater, challenges a continent away, on the rugged grasslands, mountains, and deserts of Australia, in the growing cattle and sheep industry. Like his North American equivalent, the Australian stockman rode in durable working attire—no tails and derby here. His stock saddle had a high pommel and knee pads, and he rode it loose, long in the stirrups with long reins lightly held (unlike English riding, in which the reins are held short, with tension on the horse's mouth).

On both continents, the horsemen, forced by their jobs to spend leisure as well as work time together, engaged in work-related competition on horseback for diversion—and one-upsmanship. In addition to working trained horses for their livelihood, these horsemen were required to break new horses to the saddle. The ability to do this well became a point of pride, distinguishing the great cowboy from the herd of mere competents. It also led to "bronc busting" as a game—and the foundation of rodeo.

Rodeo today is a favorite sport for western-riding fans on both continents. In addition to saddle-bronc riding, another rodeo event, calf roping, got its start from actual ranch work in the American West and Australia. Bareback bronc riding, another rodeo event on both continents, can't claim to have derived directly from ranching,

© Jim Sheldon/Visions

which entailed breaking horses to the saddle. But in its basic premise—and in its thrill quotient for spectators—it's closely related to saddle-bronc riding.

Other rodeo events include bull riding—particularly perilous—and steer wrestling (also known as bulldogging), in which the cowboy jumps down from the saddle and grabs the steer by its horn, wrestling it onto its side in a race against the clock. For American cowgirls, the rodeo event is barrel racing. Here, each contestant rides her horse in cloverleaf patterns around three oil drums, and the fastest wins.

APPENDIX

HORSE ASSOCIATIONS

AUSTRALIA

Australian Endurance Riders Association
P.O. Box 144
Nanango QLD 4615

Australian Palouse Pony Association, Inc.
P.O. Box 187
Tongala VIC 3621

Australian Quarter Horse Association
P.O. Box 979
Tamworth NSW 2340

Australian Saddle Pony Association
GPO Box 4317
Sydney NSW 2001

The Equestrian Federation of Australia
40 The Parade
P.O. Box 336
Norwood S.A. 5067

Pony Breeders and Fanciers
    Associations, Inc.
Box 54
Kangarilla S.A. 5157

Riding for the Disabled Association of
    Australia, Inc.
Royal Showgrounds
Epsom Road
Ascot Vale VIC 3032

BRITAIN

The Arab Horse Society
Windsor House
The Square
Ramsbury, Malborough
Wilts SN8 2PE

Association of British Riding Schools
Old Brewery Yard
Penzance
Cornwall TR18 2SL

British Appaloosa Society
c/o 2 Frederick Street
Rugby
Warwickshire

British Horse Society
British Equestrian Centre
Stoneleigh, Kenilworth
Warwickshire CV8 2LR

British Quarter Horse Association
4th Street
N.A.C.
Stoneleigh, Warwickshire CV8 2LG

British Show Pony Society
124 Green End Road
Sawtry
Huntington
Cambridgeshire

Clydesdale Horse Society
    of G.B. & Ireland
24 Beresford Terrace
Ayr
Ayrshire
Scotland

Dartmoor Pony Society
Fordons
17 Clare Court
New Biggin Street
Thaxted
Essex

Exmoor Pony Society
Glen Fern
Waddlcomb
Dulverton
Somerset

Horses and Ponies in Need
Glenda Spooner Trust
Emmetts Hill
Whichford
Warwickshire CV36 5PG

International League for the Protection
    of Horses
67a Camden High Street
London NW1

Racehorse Owners Association
42 Portman Square
London
W1H 9FF

Thoroughbred Breeders Association
Stansted House
The Avenue
Newmarket
Suffolk
CB8 9AA

CANADA

Alberta Paint Horse Club
RR1
Trochu, Alberta T0M 2C0

British Columbia Paint Horse Club
19507 80th
Surrey, British Columbia V3S 1P1

Canadian Cutting Horse Association
14141 Fox Drive
Edmonton, Alberta T6H 4P3

Canadian Equestrian Federation
333 River Road
Ottawa, Ontario K1L 8H9

Canadian Quarter Horse Association
360, 800 6th Avenue, S.W.
Calgary, Alberta T2P 3G3

Canadian Standardbred Horse Society
2150 Meadowvale Blvd.
Mississauga, Ontario L5N 6R6

Canadian Trotting Association
2150 Meadowvale Blvd.
Mississauga, Ontario L5N 6R6

Quarter Horse Racing Owners of Ontario
c/o Picov Downs
Hwy #2
Ajax, Ontario L1S 3B9

Quebec Quarter Horse Association
P.O. Box 39, Sation Rosemont
Montreal, Quebec H1X 3B6

United States

American Buckskin Registry Association
P.O. Box 3850
Redding, CA 96049

American Hackney Horse Society
P.O. Box 174
Pittsfield, IL 62363

American Horse Shows Association
also National Equestrian Federation
220 East 42nd St.
New York, NY 10017

American Paint Horse Association
P.O. Box 961023
Fortworth, TX 76161

American Quarter Horse Association
P.O. Box 200
Amarillo, TX 79168

American Wilderness Experience, Inc.
P.O. Box 1486
Boulder, CO 80306

Appaloosa Horse Club, Inc.
P.O. Box 8403
Moscow, ID 83843

Arabian Horse Registry of America, Inc.
12000 Zuni St.
Westminster, CO 80234

Green Mountain Horse Association, Inc.
P.O. Box 8
South Woodstock, VT 05071

International Buckskin Horse Association
P.O. Box 268
Shelby, IN 46377

International Professional Rodeo
Association
P.O. Box 645
Pauls Valley, OK 73075

International Side-Saddle Organization
P.O. Box 282
Alton Bay, NH 03810

The Jockey Club
40 East 52nd St.
New York, NY 10022

National Cutting Horse Association
4704 Highway 377 S.
Fortworth, TX 76116

National Future Farmers of America
P.O. Box 15160
Alexandria, VA 22309

Professional Rodeo Cowboys Association
101 Pro Rodeo Drive
Colorado Springs, CO 80919

Tennessee Walking Horse Breeders' and
Exhibitors' Association
P.O. Box 286
Lewisburg, TN 37091

U.S. Dressage Federation, Inc.
Box 80668
Lincoln, NB 68501

U.S. Equestrian Team, Inc.
Gladstone, NJ 07934

United States Pony Clubs
893 South Matlack St., Ste 410
West Chester, PA 19382

U.S. Trotting Association
750 Michigan Ave.
Columbus, OH 43215

Welsh Pony and Cob Society of America
P.O. Box 2977
Winchester, VA 22601